Possibility

What a Tropical Island Taught Me about

Leadership and Life

Patty Vogan

Founder of Victory Coaching

VCIPRESS

Possibility

Cover Artwork by Gillian Kirkpatrick
Interior Artwork by Sunny Dixon, Susan Dixon and Ashley Unmussig
Design and Layout by Gillian Kirkpatrick, King Graphic Design
Project Management by Karla Olson, BookStudio, Bookstudiobooks.com

Published in the United States of America by
VCI Press, 105 Avenida Del Reposo, San Clemente, CA 92672

ISBN: 978-0-9856425-0-1 (paperback)
       978-0-9856425-1-8 (epub)
       978-0-9856425-2-5 (epdf)

DEDICATION

This book is dedicated to my dad, Bob Vogan.

I close my eyes, and it feels like yesterday. It is night and I am running up and down the shore as my parents are surf fishing. Later I fall asleep in the camper to the sound of crashing waves. I remember splashing in the surf and building a wall of stones around my marvelous sand castle. The aroma of freshly perked coffee awakens me for another fun-filled day by the sea.

These memories all occurred before I was the age of five. Much to the chagrin of our mother, my brother K.C. taught me to swim before I could walk. Oh well, it all worked out as I now have salt water running through my veins and my gills get dry if I am out of the water for too long. The ocean is truly part of my soul.

I dedicate this book to the man who unlocked the treasures of the ocean for me — my dad. He first took me scuba diving when I was 12. It was the best father-daughter sport possible. We even got shiny blue baseball jackets and had "D and D Dive Team" embroidered in big letters on the back. It stood for "Dad and Daughter Dive Team," and we proudly announced that to anyone who asked. We had many adventures shore diving through the waves in Laguna Beach, finding critters under the sea. We never left each others' sides underwater. Dad was the best dive buddy ever.

It became our tradition to go to the Brig (a greasy spoon restaurant) and eat clam chowder after a morning of two tank dives off the beach. I never had the heart to tell Dad that I didn't like calm chowder; I just ate it anyway.

My dad was McGyver; he could fix or create anything. Within the first few months of my time in Tonga, my dad showed up to help out. Amen! My little sweatbox of a dive shop had no windows and nowhere to hang wetsuits. Dad to the rescue! He fixed it while I was on a dive charter. And while I was gone he talked some tourists into learning to water ski, so he set up class and off we went. From then on we taught water skiing as well as diving! Oh, why not!?!

My dad was the best salesman ever. Every year I would come back to America and go to the big dive show called DEMA. Dad would meet me there so we could work side by side selling groups on diving in Tonga. We made my first trade show booth out of PVC pipe and created a clever sign that said, "Where in the World Is Tonga?" You bet it brought people into the booth!

Dad came back to Tonga a few times and he helped roll Dolphin Diver, our 38-foot New Zealand pine boat, out of the jungle and into the sea for her maiden voyage. It took the entire village to roll the boat out on coconut logs. Then he helped to widen out the front windows and make a place for me to sit when I was driving the boat. She was a bare bones boat but strong and sturdy, like my dad.

My deep love for the ocean started with my dad. Thanks to him, every time I descend a few feet under the sea I hear the words, "Welcome home." The ocean is my home town and my place of stability. My adventuresome spirit also came from Dad, and I learned to discover the possibilities in many situations growing up.

I am forever grateful, Dad, that you introduced me to my true love, the ocean.

ACKNOWLEDGMENTS

I've been writing and rewriting this story for years, because, I think, I haven't really wanted to write this part. I don't have the best memory, you see, and I am so afraid of forgetting someone. So maybe I should just start with, "I am so sorry I forgot to mention you."

This book was in my brain for a long time before it ever hit the paper, and there are many people to thank who supported me to get it there.

Thank you to God for showing up in my life even when I thought He was not there and giving me His grace over and over again. I am so blessed.

My mom is gone so she won't know I thanked her, but out of respect it is important that I do. Thank you, Mom, for teaching me to openly hug, love, and trust everyone.

My dad is the key that unlocked all the treasures of the ocean for me. That is why I am dedicating this book to him. He taught me to scuba dive at age 12. I was lucky enough to read the dedication to him as he died just before the book was published.

My best friend of 25 plus years came to see me in Tonga. Terry Rifkin and her husband, Chris Hawn, came and we went sailing and fishing to our hearts' delight. I'll never forget the quadruple strike of yellowfin tuna. Reel it in girl! Terry has been my rock and the best friend anyone could ever ask for in one lifetime. Chris is my biggest fan.

Thank you to the cast of characters, fruit loops, land sharks, friends, and lovers that inspired all the South Pacific adventures in my life. Don't stop the carnival!

To the people who have put up with me talking about this book and listening to me read them a section or asking what they thought about this or that. You have all been so kind; thank you for your love, support, ideas, and advice.

Bill Arcudi, Neil Burns, Susan Dixon, Bob & Cyndi Elders, Denise Eldredge, Dwight & Suzanne Frindt, Bobby Lynn Gileno, Scott Jones, Ada Koch, Mark Fox, Chris Hawn, Allison Haynes, Ryan Heuser, Martha Hoffman, John Boy Nielson, Lynne McVean, Terry Rifkin, Sheri Roberts, Penney Vaughn.

A special thank you to my boyfriend, Mike Geyer, for his love and for putting his life on hold to help me make this book — and the dreams attached to it — become a reality.

Taylor Hartman, Ph.D., Author of The Color Code
Bob McKnight, CEO, Quiksilver
Rafael Pastor, Chairman of Vistage International
Rick Warren, Pastor, Saddleback Church

Victory Coaching Clients
Victory Coaching Staff

My Vistage International CEO 3303 Group
My Vistage International Key Executive 9074 Group
My Vistage International Chair 6003 Group

Editors are a blessing in life for people like me who have a huge admiration for their talents. Thanks to a few editor friends and professionals who got me through the process: thank you Michele Whiteaker for helping me deliver my thoughts onto paper, Kaci Slymen, first draft edits, and Claire Gerus for guiding me to Karla Olson.

Karla Olson from BookStudio shepherded me through the rewrites and the publishing process. Thank you to Gillian Kirkpatrick of King Graphic Design for getting us through the delicate task of book design, Ashley Unmussig and Sunny Dixon and Susan Dixon for inside artwork.

Last but not least ... Puddy Tat, my furry little friend who sat by my side for hours as I wrote.

TABLE OF CONTENTS

PROLOGUE

There's usually a catalyst . . . a pivotal event that makes you realize you want something more. Some of us push aside this passionate feeling of unfulfilled possibility. We put it off as unrealistic or discount it as impossible, often before we've done the first bit of research or even reflected on the idea.

Where's the fun in life if there isn't possibility?

In the Jimmy Buffett–Herman Wouk musical, *Don't Stop the Carnival*, Governor Alton Sanders asks, "Have you ever dreamed of escaping from your dull existence to a new life on a tropical island?"

I didn't just think about the possibility. I seized it.

In the middle of a successful marketing career, I moved to the South Pacific, to the Kingdom of Tonga, and opened a scuba diving business.

I'll bet you have a similar fantasy in your life, a possibility you fantasize about. It might be opening your own business, taking your business to the next level, or pursuing a new hobby or activity. Whether you think of this dream every day or only once in a while, why wait to make your dream come true? Why not discover the power of Possibility Thinking today?

I did. I lived in the warm tropics and operated my business for seven years—an actual dream come true.

What Is Possibility Thinking?
It is sad, but true, that most people have dreams they never pursue. Instead, they let all sorts of outside influences derail their dreams.

As founder and president of Victory Coaching International and chairperson of Vistage International, my team and I coach CEOs and leaders from all walks of life to tangibly improve their business success. We help them become better leaders by teaching them to make improved decisions; therefore, we obtain greater results. We are especially interested in teaching transformational self-awareness in leadership skills and team development. Even though I'm serious about our subject matter, my coaching style is rather laid-back—island style. A friend and client, Bob McKnight, CEO of Quiksilver, once said, "If you're not having fun, who wants to learn?" I try to make sure that my clients have fun while they learn.

Although I have a Master's Degree in Psychological Sciences, my background is far richer from life experiences than from any textbook or class. My lifetime of undersea encounters is the inspiration for this book. As you will discover, while in the tropics, I learned the importance of striving for balance in life. As a coach, I encourage my clients to live their lives and run their businesses by design and not by default.

What's In It for You?

This story is not about moving to the tropics; it's about living a life of few or no regrets. You are never too old to discover something new about yourself and find ways to use your God-given gifts. I didn't want to be ninety-five years old, sitting on the deck of my sailboat, sipping a gin martini, and doing the "shoulda-woulda-coulda" dance. I want to make sure that you don't, either.

What will you get from following me on this journey? In my everyday life and coaching, I use the lessons I learned from facing challenges and gaining leadership experience in Tonga. The best way for me to share the lessons learned—from seven years of living there—is through my crazy stories. When I meet someone or work to inspire through my presentations, my stories have a message in them. Find the message for you.

The life, love, and leadership lessons are woven throughout the stories. Sometimes, I tell you what I learned from the experience, and sometimes I don't. The benefits you glean will be up to your own discovery.

That is my wish for you . . . discovery. May you uncover the possibility in your life, as well as the leadership skills and practices, and may you see them from a new perspective, as reflected in the stories of my journey. Find the courage to try to face a different kind of possibility for yourself than you have ever tried before. You really can live your life's possibility. May you discover your Possibility Thinking and recognize how quick and easy it is to apply Possibility Thinking to your life. The moment you learn to flip the switch to Possibility Thinking, your life will change dramatically.

Your Possibility

"Victory over one's self is the greatest victory of all."

This is one of my quotes, inspired by one of my dad's favorite quotes by University of Notre Dame football coach, Lou Holtz. Why does this quote resonate with leaders? Once they become aware of how they can get in their own way—and then learn to move through their ego and pride to get to the other side—they experience epiphanies and gain victory over themselves. Life's possibilities become clearer for them. We all have natural talents and gifts we can use to better ourselves, our families, and our world. If we are not keenly aware of these natural talents and gifts, then we cannot use them. That's why opening yourself up to your possibilities is so important.

Our deepest fear is not that we are inadequate. Our deepest fear is that we are powerful beyond measure. It is our light, not our darkness that most frightens us. We ask ourselves, Who am I to be brilliant, gorgeous, talented, fabulous? Actually, who are you not to be? You are a child of God. Your playing small does not serve the world. There is nothing enlightened about shrinking so that other people won't feel insecure around you. We are all meant to shine, as children do. We were born to make manifest the glory of God that is within us. It's not just in some of us; it's in everyone. And as we let our own light shine, we unconsciously give other people permission to do the same. As we are liberated from our own fear, our presence automatically liberates others.

—Marianne Williamson
A Return to Love

VOGANISM

You're never too cool or too old to learn something new, laugh harder, live fuller, and love deeper.

One of my gifts is enthusiasm. I remember often getting trophies and recognition awards on a sports team when I was a child, not for being M.V. P. (Most Valuable Player), but for being "most enthusiastic." That made me cringe when I was a kid. I was not a cheerleader and did not want to be labeled one. My enthusiasm didn't seem like a gift to me; it was just me being me. It wasn't until far into my adulthood that I realized enthusiasm is a special quality that I could use to help others and myself. In fact, I understand now that it is an integral part of my Possibility Thinking.

Being enthusiastic about the things that are true to my soul is easy for me. For instance, inspiring others to protect our oceans is a natural way for me to use my gift. Another one of my core values and beliefs is that all people on this planet are leaders; they just might not be aware of it yet. Walking the path of discovery with my clients is an exciting journey for me. I love to be a partner in their self-discovery and watch them see their possibility.

Discover POSSIBILITY Thinking

This lesson is about allowing yourself to discover the possibility in your life, instead of being stopped by all the responsibilities and misgivings you think you have.

· ·

Scuba divers know that shark attacks happen; yet, knowing they happen doesn't keep them out of the water. On a calm and glassy sea, our dive boat floated miles off shore in the Tonga Trench. The sun shone warmly on a perfect tropical day in paradise. The water, gin clear and the deepest blue, displayed the most enchanted invitation for water play with its sunbeam apex. Mother Ocean beckoned. So, why did I hesitate? Why did I feel so much fear? Did I recognize the distant echo of mythological Sirens drawing me into danger?

After snorkeling and photographing in the water for longer than an hour, I knew I had captured award-winning shots of dolphins and humpback whales. I was relaxing for a moment, floating in the water, when I saw it: aggressive posturing from the depths. The man-eating deadly kind … with me as its target.

This lesson is an intricate part of my leadership development and my goal to help others discover Possibility Thinking. I'll pick it back up again later in the book after laying out a few possibility lessons.

We've established that I'm fond of jumping in with both feet. Sure, it's generally off of the swim step of a boat holding my mask on my face with my fins slapping the ocean's surface. More often, I sneak into the underwater world from the edge of a dinghy, rolling backwards with hardly a splash. The destination is always the same: somewhere deeper than where I started.

To understand my story, you'll first need an introduction to Tonga. I can tell you all sorts of details about Tonga. For instance, it's located at 175° west longitude and 20° south latitude in the South Pacific Islands, close to the islands of Fiji. It's a kingdom. Yes, the island is ruled by a king. In fact, it's the last ancient Polynesian kingdom in the world, and it is the only island nation in the region that has never been colonized.

No matter what I tell you, you'll still probably imagine it as something familiar. A more remote Hawaii with fewer tourists. And I'll let you go ahead and think that, for now. You would be right about the warm azure waters, crystal blue skies, and lush emerald green vegetation making for the perfect tropical paradise. It's a playground for scuba divers, sailing enthusiasts, and people fishing for sport. That's why we chose it for our honeymoon.

For the sake of my story, let's call my newlywed husband Superman. He looks like he's jumped right out of a Marvel comic book or swooped off of the big screen to land in my life. We want to spend our honeymoon sailing, but we both stink at navigation. So, we pick Tonga because the brochures say it has fifty islands within sight of each other for bathtub sailing. We'll be able to see land from all destinations and, therefore, navigate our way home. At the very least, we'll be able to pull into the closest anchorage while we wait for help. Tonga has the added benefit of being far, far away from my hectic position as Director of Marketing in a hospital. Unlike the possibility when I'm in Hawaii, there's no way they can phone me there.

We spend two heavenly weeks sailing around these idyllic islands and diving in water with 200-foot visibility. It's amazing. I'm living my dream. We go scuba diving among beautiful sea creatures, like jellyfish, clownfish, and brightly colored soft and hard corals. The deep-red-colored soft corals are neighbored by the largest yellow sea fans I've ever seen. The water is so clear it is like looking through air. If you can call it bathtub sailing, then you might as well call it tropical aquarium diving. The fish display themselves in brilliant varieties. The hard and soft coral look as though they've arrived just off of the pages of *National Geographic*.

I'm truly more comfortable under the water than above it. This is especially true for me in Tonga. Every time I get in the water to dive, a "welcome home" feeling takes over my senses as I descend. I feel like every animal in the sea is speaking only to me. And all of them are happy to see me again! Life doesn't get much better than this!

After a day of exquisite diving, we join a group of salty dogs sitting in The Sand Bar, discussing life and solving all the worlds' problems over bottles of home-brewed Royal Tongan beer. I'm used to this scene from a lifetime among boaters. Sharing a beer and sea stories are truly part of the culture. As always happens toward end of the evening, the conversation turns philosophical. A question hangs in the fresh island air, just begging for an answer.

"If you could do what you really wanted to do in life, what would it be? It doesn't matter if you have the right education or the money or any of that stuff. What would you do?" asks Tomasi, the manager of the Moorings Yacht Charter Company, where we rented our floating home for two weeks. Tomasi looks at me and says, "Well… ?"

My mind zips back a couple of decades: I'm diving with my dad off of Laguna Beach. The tourists are gone. Locals beach comb and play basketball. Gulls flit from streetlight to streetlight. This gray day seeps from the clouds, melding to the horizon and sewing a seam to the sea. Underwater, my 12-year-old gaze spots brilliant orange flashes darting among the kelp. Much more prevalent are the dull opaleyes and schools of silver bait fish.

Still, I'm with my dad. And what can be better than the weightlessness? The floating? The freedom? Feeling the connection. I'm trying not to think about my hands, numb under the neoprene, or how cold my ears will feel when I peel off my hood. The dive done, I back out of the surf behind Dad, pulling off my fins, and racing toward the towels. The faster I get my gear off and get dry, the faster my body warms up. I don't even bother taking off my bathing suit before jamming into my sweatpants and hooded sweatshirt while dancing in place. Dad loads the cart with the tanks, wetsuits, and weight belts. We'll hose the salt water off when we get home.

He's walking ahead of me, and I'm wiping my runny nose with my beach towel. My starfish-purple lips struggle to remain closed, jarred by my chattering teeth. I shout ahead into the wind, "Someday, Dad, I'm going to have a dive shop in the tropics where the water is clear, beautiful, and WARM!"

Back in the present, without thinking, I say, "I've always wanted to have a scuba diving shop in the tropics, where it's really warm."

Tomasi raises one eyebrow and says, "Well, why don't you do that here, and do it now?"

I mumble something back like, "Well, I… ahhh… errr… am next in line for VP of

Marketing, blah, blah, blah…!"

"Oh, I get it," Tomasi says with a sarcastic flair. "You are one of those people who talk about your dreams but never make them come true!"

The hair on the back of my neck stands straight out; my posture becomes erect as I turn and look down on him. "No, that is not true!"

"Okay, then, do it here. If you bring in a professional scuba diving business, and do it up right, I will support you and give you all of the Moorings' clients — and not even charge a percentage." Later that night, under the star-laden sky of Tonga, I lie on the deck of our sailboat and contemplate life as I count the satellites and shooting stars moving at a steady pace across the sky. The Southern Cross quickly becomes my comforting friend.

The sunrise is just as stunning as the sunset the night before. Over a hot cup of dark and steamy Tongan coffee, I say to my new husband, "I want to build a scuba diving business. It's my dream, and I want to do it. I know we're on our honeymoon, but I'm not kidding, I really want to make my dream come true. I don't want to be old and looking back, saying I wish I would have at least tried! What do you think?"

Superman thinks for a moment before saying, "Why not? It sounds like fun; let's do it!" ■

VOGANISM

Discover
POSSIBILITY
Thinking.

POSSIBILITY Coaching Session

We are sitting in my office for a coaching session. I've just told you this story, and your response is, "Yeah, nice story, but I already own a business that I love. I have a mortgage, kids, and too much responsibility to go do something crazy like that!" I understand, and I am not encouraging you to run away to a tropical island. The purpose of the story is to help you get in touch with desires and passions that might be buried. They could be dreams you have for your business, your family, or your life.

I would start by asking you these questions:

Think back to when you were a child. What did you want to do when you grew up? Why was this goal exciting to you? How did it make you feel? What are you doing today that gives you similar feelings?

Young children generally don't have responsibilities or life experiences that get in the way of their dreams. When you were a young child, anything was possible. That's why you said you wanted to be a firefighter or an astronaut or a cloud photographer. You weren't stopped in your tracks because you had to pay the mortgage, live up to others' expectations, or support your family.

Once you've recaptured the excitement of being an innocent child, I would ask you to look at your life today with the same possibility and enthusiasm. That's when I would ask you:

If you could be anything, have anything, change anything in your life today, what would it be?

Don't hold back. Think big. Think bold. Think possible. Don't filter at all; just tell me what would make you feel very happy and fulfilled. What would make you passionate?

Okay, now let's create possibilities. Once again, I would ask you to go back to your childhood.

Who supported you in your dreams? How was this support given?

Maybe it was your mother or grandfather who said, "Little one, dream big and make it happen; you can do whatever you want to do." Maybe it was your dad who said, "Go for it; you're amazing." Remember how those words made you feel, and try to hold onto that.

But now, I would have to ask you: Who squashed your dreams? How were your dreams squashed?

We all have someone in our lives — perhaps several someones or you, yourself — who says, "That's a great dream, but it's just that, a dream. Get real, kid." Figure out what the triggers are that squash your Possibility Thinking. Then take a careful look at those triggers and determine whether or not they are really obstacles for you.

The purpose of this exercise is to get you back in touch with the passion and enthusiasm of Possibility Thinking, and to filter out the negatives that inevitably come rushing in. Instead, leave yourself open to exploring the possibilities. In the end, they might turn out to be unrealistic, but I can guarantee you will find something that will work for you, something that you hadn't thought was a possibility before.

LESSON 2

PERSEVERANCE Trumps Logic

Have you been at a place in business or life — or are you currently at that place — when you've felt as if all the odds are against you and you really just want to quit? We have all been there. However, if you are like me, something inside you pushes you on, and you persevere.

What is perseverance? Perseverance can be viewed through its namesake, *Perseverance*, an early steam locomotive built by Timothy Burstall in the early 1800's. Perseverance broke down on the way to the Rainhill trials, and Burstall spent the first five days of the contest trying to repair the locomotive. He finally got it running on the sixth and final day, but was only able to achieve a speed of six mph. For his perseverance, Burstall was awarded a consolation prize of £25!

Sometimes, when your back is against the wall, visualize this "little train that could" and its creator. You, too, can choose to keep on going. This lesson is about perseverance and its importance in business.

· ·

After we return from our honeymoon trip, it takes an additional eighteen months to get all our ducks in order. I continue working as Director of Marketing at the hospital, becoming acutely aware of how many people use the slightest obstacle as an excuse for why they "can't" do this or that.

When an obstacle appears, many people stop in their tracks. It is far easier to use the obstacle as an excuse than it is to persevere. When I hear the word *no*, I immediately interpret this as an acronym; *NO* stands for "Not Obvious." To me, the acronym says that the value of what I'm doing is just not obvious yet to the person who said *no*. Therefore, my job is to communicate the value I see in another way.

I stop thinking about Tonga as a tropical paradise and quickly realize it's going to be a daunting place to launch a business. First, I need to obtain proper licenses before making my move. I've heard of some foreigners upending their whole lives and moving to the island, intending to start a business, but failing to first obtain required licenses, a situation that made the "powers-that-be" mad and resulted in the foreigners never being permitted to practice chosen professions on Tongan soil. I take note of those before me who tried to work a shortcut through the system. They lost everything they owned and everything they dreamed of. The stories about their personalities portray them as excessively demanding, demeaning, and downright nasty. The Tongan people are very proud and very loving, and I can't say that I blame them for kicking out the expats. I know that I certainly don't want to put myself in that predicament.

 After moving forward to take care of licenses, I make sure my work visa is in place. I get my business and development licenses in writing before going, since the development license allows me to enter the country with a tax and duty rate that is 50 percent lower than the rate of a visitor. That's a huge monetary boost for someone building a business. Besides, it lets the customs officials know I'm legitimate and not just a dumb blonde from America.

The communication tools available to me are phone and fax; the Internet isn't adequately up and running in the Kingdom. Tonga's status as a royalty-run, third-world country definitely figures into my preparations. We are quick to make plans on our end, but Tonga is slow to respond on its side. Remember, Tonga was never colonized by Europeans. It is their right to make up the rules that suit the Kingdom.

After faxing the Tongan government twenty-five times to request approval for our paperwork, we get a fax back. It says, *"Mr. Fale Kavacoupu out of country. Maybe back next week."* I wonder if the last sentence is meant to have a question mark instead of a period.

Many times, I think of calling it quits. I am haunted by that voice in my head: *You are one of those people who talk about your dreams and never make them come true!* I remind myself that if this were easy, there would be dive businesses on every corner, just as there are in Hawaii. This is not easy, not Hawaii, and I am determined to persevere until I am told *NO*. And then I will just try another way.

This process goes on and on and on. It becomes a game, one I don't intend to lose. The record is forty-three days of faxing without receiving a response. Giving up seems the logical thing to do after faxing more than 100 times with no answer. Not even a *maybe* — well, okay, one *maybe*. However, perseverance trumps logic. I am not going to give up.

Finally, my perseverance pays off, and we get the go-ahead for the business!

Another obstacle is that I do not have a scuba instructor license; in fact, I've never been an instructor. Considering that I've been scuba diving since I was twelve years old and leading dives in places like California, Mexico, and Hawaii, getting my instructor license is a piece of cake. But then there's Superman. He learned to dive a month before our honeymoon sailing trip to Tonga, so he needs a lot more practice, which takes more time than he wants to put in. He has the I-want-what-I-want-and-I-want-it-now syndrome, which is the opposite of "perseverance trumps logic."

Superman manages to pass his coursework and become an instructor with the absolute minimum real-life diving experience. He eventually proves to be more dangerous than he's worth underwater, but that is a story for another time. Let's just say he almost killed himself and others with his lack of experience and poor decision-making. Actually, I think he wins the award for my being most outrageously angry with another human! With the frustrating dealings with the Tongan government behind us, we tackle the necessities of acquiring the needed funds and buying all the equipment. We consult with experts regarding how to best set up shop. One of the most helpful is the man who works for the compressor company. During three separate meetings, we draw plans that cover how to build a dive station and connect the hoses and compressor. He teaches me how to fill the tanks and change the filter system. Then he makes me put it all together in front of him over and over. He's a great teacher. I've never filled a scuba tank or worked in a dive shop. I am pretty much as green as they come, and he ends up being as kind and patient as they come.

The Dolphin Pacific Diving shop will be housed in a dismantled Sears' backyard tin shed, which we'll bring with us from the U.S. and bolt to a foundation. So, we pack up as many dive supplies as we can fit inside the 20' x 20' shipping container, cramming our meager personal belongings in the leftover spaces. In addition to the tin shed, I decide we need: twelve sets of gear, twelve regulators, twenty-six tanks, twenty-eight tank valves, eighteen buoyancy compensators from XS to XL, thirty masks, thirty snorkels, thirty sets of fins, repair kits galore, a huge commercial compressor, a mini back-up compressor, five sets of waterskis, ropes, life vests, assorted tools, five windsurfer boards and sails, a Toyota truck, and a partridge in a pear tree.

I don't have much to bring personally, since I gave away all my Armani business suits and high heels. I'm planning to live a barefoot life on the beach with only three bathing suits, five pair of long shorts (showing knees not allowed), and a huge box of professionally embossed logo polo shirts to wear and sell. A uniform every day takes the decision away! Can't forget the pink flip-flops for more formal occasions.

Little do I know, my education on perseverance has only just begun. The International Date Line crosses right by Tonga; hence, its nickname: The Land Where Time Stands Still. I jump on the plane to Tonga alone, with plans for Superman to wrap up things in the states and join me in six weeks. My family and friends are not happy with my decision to travel alone to a foreign country to set up the business. To me, it sounds like a fun adventure.

Appropriately, I leave on the Fourth of July. Independence Day. ■

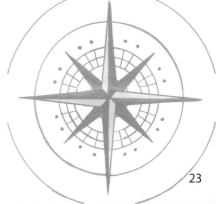

POSSIBILITY Coaching Session

No matter what type of difficult situation you are encountering, your internal attitude and outward actions in addressing it will make all the difference in your success, failure, and perseverance. These will all factor into your decision to quit or choose a new direction. One of my favorite quotes sits on my best friend's desk.

If you think you can or think you can't, either way you are right!
—Henry Ford

We so often overlook the power of the mind over our body, attitude, and actions. But often thought, not action, is the key to moving forward or standing still. Remember, if you think you can, you will. If you think you can't, well, then you won't.

Here are some questions to ask yourself when you are trying to decide between quitting and persevering:

• What is driving you to persevere through this difficult time?

• Who is supporting or not supporting your desire to quit? A drive to quit or persevere can sometimes be due to a strong influence from others and not just an internal thought.

• If you persevere or quit today, describe how that will affect your future?

• Where are you going to get the energy to persevere?

Accountability to yourself and/or a partner can be a huge help in providing the courage and energy to keep going. My former husband, Superman, was very good at encouraging me to continue and persevere when I was close to throwing in the towel many times. For us, we turned getting the license into a game and made it fun instead of wallowing in the discouragement that arose from the lack of response from the Tongan government after daily contact.

This is a perfect example of how perseverance trumps logic. We could have said that it was obvious the Tongans didn't want us. Instead, we kept sending the fax until we got the response we desired.

VOGANISM

No person, place or thing

can drive you crazy unless

you give up the keys.

Rats and RESEARCH

Have you ever felt so right about something that it would never even occur to you to slow down and reflect or do some research about the decision? Most people need to listen to their intuition more frequently, but many entrepreneurs tend to shoot first and aim later. Sometimes, even when your gut tells you that you are right on target or that the bad consequences of something will never happen, you may be surprised if you forge ahead.

This lesson's story is about the importance of taking time to reflect about your decision and support it with research when starting a new company or making an important decision. The ideas here apply to all areas of business and life, especially when you are facing something that is not familiar to you.

. . . .

"A toast." Jeff raises his third glass of Tongan beer at the dinner table.

I don't need a drink. The jet lag leaves me with a buzz more potent than beer. Over Jeff's shoulder, I spy my bed for the night—a sheet draped over the cushions on the rattan couch. Jeff is an Australian boatbuilder who, along with his wife and two kids, calls Tonga home. We've gotten to know each other long distance since I bought my dive boat, *Surface Interval*, from him. Those throw pillows sure look inviting—and they appear to be the only stationary objects in the room. I try to focus.

Jeanine, Jeff's wife, and their two kids invite me to try some Vegemite spread on my bread.

It looks like axle grease and smells worse. From reading the label, I figure out it's a Kraft product manufactured in Australia. How bad can it be? Minding my manners, I spread a bit on my bread and take a bite. My face goes into contortions of: "Yuck! What is that?" They all laugh, and so do I. I missed my research on that one. Oops!

POSSIBILITY COACHING TIP:

Believe it or not, after many years, I've acquired a taste for Vegemite. In fact, there's some in my refrigerator right now. Vegemite will always serve as a metaphor to me for not immediately dismissing something new because I don't like it. When I realize I am in an area foreign to me, I make sure I don't shun it right away, but rather pause and give it a chance. This is helpful in business systems and in decisions regarding hiring and firing people. When I manage to miss the research part . . . all is not lost. I remember to question whether the potential employee might just grow on me. In following this lesson, keep your mind available for opportunity by leaving space for growth.

When I keep my thoughts open to the possibility that there is more than one way to look at something, accepting the tenet that there might be more than one truth or one path leading to the same goal, this helps me stay, say, and act with an open mind. It's been proven to me over and over again just how much I can learn from others when I stay open for longer than I am generally comfortable staying open. My greatest growth opportunities have come when I've allowed myself to be uncomfortable.

Jeff lives on the main island called Nuku'alofa. Once my container arrives, I will make my way from here to the smaller northern group of islands and the village of Vava'u to build my new life and business. It takes a 75-minute flight aboard a Twin Otter aircraft to travel from one island to the other.

"To the new captain of *Surface Interval*," Jeff toasts.

I roll my eyes and cock my head to the side with an appreciative smirk. "Well, thanks Jeff . . . " I begin, before being cut off by Jeff.

"May she survive her voyage and bring you health, wealth, and happiness," Jeff finishes.

"I put my vote in for that" is all I can manage.

After I pick my way through the simple dinner, Jeanine eventually gathers the dishes and heads the kids toward the kitchen, leaving Jeff and me alone.

"So, tomorrow, we meet the boat at the harbor . . . should it still be afloat." Jeff seems to think this is funny, but I see no humor. My storage shed with all my belongings is my anchor in this floaty, jet-laggy place. I'm separated from it by the travel time and a lengthy customs process.

I feel a nudge of excitement break through the blur of my internal time clock telling me to go to bed. We square away all the details. Jeff will have men there to help; all I'll need to do is to direct them as to which items go to boxes labeled House or Dive Shop.

"You've got nothing to worry about," he reassures me after ducking into the kitchen to retrieve another beer. "Oh, and you don't have anything illegal, do you?"

"Noooo. Not me. Nothing."

"So, no drugs, guns, anything?" He sits down.

"Huh?"

"What's 'huh?' supposed to mean?"

POSSIBILITY COACHING TIP:

When passion fuels ideas, putting the cart before the horse can be very easy. When we own our own businesses, we often don't have anyone to answer to or use as a sounding board for important business decisions. That's why doing research is so important—a lesson I learned the hard way.

I didn't do enough research on the country itself before moving to the Kingdom of Tonga, which means I learned this particular lesson through the School of Hard Knocks. Do you think gun laws might be important to research when you are moving to a new country? I had no idea that Tonga was gun free. After arriving, I learned that even police officers didn't carry guns. I had grown up in a family of hunters and peace officers and military veterans who taught their little sister to shoot. You know, the Annie Oakley thing? By the way, I'm a really good shot! So I naturally took my Colt .38 to Tonga.

"I'm a woman alone in a new world. I brought my gun."

Jeff does not see the humor.

Now, if you were the king of a country that didn't allow guns and someone new arrived with such a weapon, what would you do? Well, in Tonga, the culture tends to take a no-tolerance approach.

"You're going to jail, Patty."

"What?!!"

"There are no guns allowed here. If they find your gun, you are going to jail." Jeff paced the living room while he harangued me. "Do you know what you've done? I could go to jail, too. I could lose my business!" I'll spare you the expletives, which bring his wife back into the room with clucks of disapproval at my ignorance.

All I can do is shrug my shoulders and raise my hands in apology. I keep repeating, "I'm sorry; I didn't know." It's a mistake I can't wish away. Then I come up with, "What do I do?"

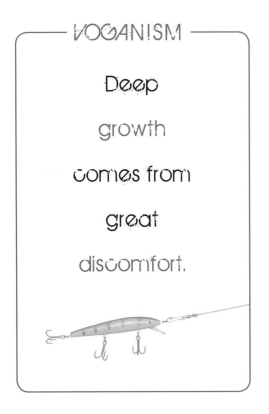

VOGANISM

Deep

growth

comes from

great

discomfort.

Jeff stops pacing and looks at his wife. She raises her eyebrows and shakes her head. He thinks for a good while. I withstand the angry glares.

Jeff points his index finger, giving the naughty-child warning. "You are going to learn to cry when I tell you—and you'd better learn it quick." With that, he stomps off into the bedroom. Jeanine has already left the room, and now I'm alone and in a panic. I curse the whole situation, but climb into my pajamas, figuring he'll explain more when he's calmed down.

My sudden hysterical screams bring Jeff and his wife running back out. Something is in my pajamas, wiggling and skittering around. Ahhhh, it's a rat! A little mouse runs out one leg of my PJs as my anxiety attack reaches full tilt. Once Jeff and Jeanine figure out I'm not in any mortal danger, as my screams might indicate, they return to their bedroom without a word. It's a wonder I get any sleep at all that night.

The next morning, Jeff takes me to the Chief of Police. I stand silently by while Jeff explains that I'm a stupid American girl, that I didn't know the law and made a big mistake. I brought a gun into the country, and it is inside the container—just arrived on the dock the day before and not yet cleared customs. He pleads with the Chief of Police to have pity on me and not put me in jail. Hmmm . . . that is my cue.

The crocodile tears start rolling down my face.

I had been worried enough the night before at Jeff's, but apparently, the reality hadn't hit until I stood next to the Chief of Police and found that he wasn't budging. Jail! Are you kidding? Are they going to put me in jail and throw away the key? Yes, they can—and yes, they will. The tears are not an act; I'm thinking I'm history, and so is my dream.

Do the tears work? No. The officials are still going to put me in jail! Jeff talks them into waiting to arrest me until the container has been unloaded. So, the Police Chief and Customs Agents stand by, inspecting, as Jeff and I unload every item from the 20x20 shipping container.

Lucky and unlucky for me, I also brought cases of wine. I know I'm in for it when I put my hands on the bottles, packed two at a time and wrapped tightly in brown packing paper. They come off a bit too Miami Vice and reminiscent of tightly packed kilos of drugs. I just know my popularity is diminishing quickly! But I hope the absence of drugs will play to my advantage.

Here's where another lesson—and the "lucky" part of the story—come in: Never forget that a smile is a universal tool. A kind, honest smile speaks volumes in any language. So, I smile my brightest, whitest smile at the Tongan police, carefully unwrap the brown paper packages, and hand each man a bottle of wine and say, in my best broken Tongan, "Gift for you." Then I smile again, uncork some of California's finest Chardonnay, and toast.

Never underestimate the power of a smile; it kept me out of jail. Well, maybe the wine helped, too. ■

POSSIBILITY Coaching Session

Each country has its own culture. Each industry has its own culture; each company has its own company culture. And each department within a company has its own culture. There are many unspoken rules in companies and departments. Doing a little bit of research on the "not-so-obvious" can prove to be very important when you are deciding how to work within a department, a company, or an industry.

I missed an important step in the life of an entrepreneur. Research is not just for the laboratories of scientific studies and rats. When entrepreneurs get new ideas for turning a profit or fueling their passions, they'll find that moving too quickly and missing an important step in research can be very costly—and scary.

When you find yourself facing something that is not completely familiar, here are a few questions to ask yourself:

• Who else has done something like this, someone I can talk to so I can learn more?

• Who can I ask about different decisions that could have been made? Who is an expert on this subject, someone I can turn to as I work to discover what I might be missing?

• What would my competition do?

- After I research what my competition does well, I can ask myself how I could do it just as well. It's the same in reverse. When I see where my competition is missing the mark, how will I fill that void?

- Right now, is my decision based more on gut-level feelings or research?

The most important parts of this lesson relate to being open enough to admit that you don't know everything and having the courage to ask questions.

LESSON 4

Embrace Your F.E.A.R.

Many entrepreneurs and business owners do everything they can to avoid being controlled by others. We want to be "in charge" of our own destinies and our own actions and decisions. No one can tell us what to do or not to do. Therefore, always being in control becomes one of the most important factors in our daily lives. In fact, being your own boss in everything you do is so much a part of your DNA that you don't even realize just how controlling you are—until it hits you smack in the face that it is impossible to control everybody and everything. That's when you have to admit that always needing to be in the driver's seat can actual cause you to make the wrong choices.

I hope you are open enough to ask yourself a very important question right now. If you are, read on. The question is: *Am I letting my need to control affect the way I act as a leader and a person?*

Things feel out of control when you are going against the flow of events that are occurring. There is always more than one way or direction to get to a result. When events are not progressing in the direction you think is the "right" one, you naturally want to redirect and take stronger control of the situation. However, when you are open to being in the flow, you open yourself to possibilities that exist beyond your control—and that can be a really good thing! Think about how a sailor uses the wind to get to the intended destination. The sailor goes with the flow of the wind and current, not against it. In fact, half the time, the sailor must travel in a direction that seems totally wrong in order to get to the intended destination. It feels irrational, but as any sailor knows, it is the only way.

There's no denying it: Entrepreneurs and business owners like to be in control. That's why they are the heads of companies. As one entrepreneurial friend of mine said, "I can't just sit in the cockpit of the sailboat; I have to be the captain. I cannot control the wind, but I can always adjust my sails."

In most cases, we make smart, rational decisions that keep our endeavors moving in a forward and upward direction. Occasionally, all leaders find themselves in difficult situations. The feeling that something is going wrong creeps down from our brains and starts to make our throats constrict and our hearts pound, and we just have to reach out and grab the wheel. Sometimes, we make decisions to use the force of the wind, and other times, we fight against it.

What is it that makes us feel crazy when we are not in control? I say it's F.E.A.R.:

- False
- Evidence
- Appearing
- Real

Sometimes, F.E.A.R. can be so stealthy that we don't even realize we are being controlled by it. It's hard to feel its deadly grip when we are in the middle of a business meeting and we just want to get things done and move on.

When has fear controlled you without your realizing it? Believe it or not, this happens to everyone. If you cannot think of an example, maybe the story below will help you see things about yourself insofar as F.E.A.R. getting in your way as you work to serve as a leader.

. . . .

My body and emotions hover close to exhaustion after I'm forced to repack my strewn cargo into smaller wooden crates just to put it on the Inter-island Ferry. All I can think about is how long the trip on the ferry boat will be and if I will see my dolphin friends on the ride. That's when Jeff, the boatbuilder, informs me that the ferry's nickname is the *Floating Coffin*. Is this another sign that I've made the biggest mistake of my life? Jeff guides me in a different direction and encourages me to take a 75-minute flight, instead. I watch everything I own, plus my new boat, float out to sea with pigs, chickens, goats, and seasick locals.

My adventure is in real time now. I'm the star in my own movie. I'm feeling a bit seasick myself and fearful, due to all the unexpected almost-catastrophes I've faced already. This is a far cry from my blissful daydream of azure seas and dancing dolphins.

For the next two days, I wait with fearful anxiety for my belongings to arrive, trying to settle into my new rental home, despite its lack of a toilet. The sun sets as the *Olova'a*, and my "new life" belongings round the mountain and start up the channel to the harbor where I'm standing. I feel victorious, like the little girl who finally fits the last piece into her first big puzzle. As the ferry slowly makes its way up the channel, I notice it's leaning to the right. I fear it's about to sink before my eyes. But then I realize that the Tongans on the boat are leaning over the rails on the right side of the ferry, waving to the people in the village.

POSSIBILITY COACHING TIP:

My fears are getting in the way of my focus, and my outlook is becoming more negative by the minute. As you will see, I will soon become controlling and inefficient. Sound familiar? How do you respond when your emotions have been hijacked by negative thoughts?

As all the seasick locals, animals, and wooden crates are unloaded from the ferry, I stand at the dock and watch workers place worn and tattered straps on my boat to lift it with a crane that looks like it has been around since the 1800s. I swear! I assume, in my infinite wisdom, that this very small group of islands doesn't have boats delivered very often, if ever. The majority of boats in the Vava'u group of islands are small wooden fishing boats, built locally, or world cruisers from far-away countries. It's obvious to me, in my heightened negative state, that I need to control and fix all the people on the island, because they are doing it all wrong. I'm sure you can relate to that thought, too: *They are doing it all wrong!* I'm sure they will drop my boat, splintering it into a thousand fiberglass slivers. I board the ferry in a huff, trying my hardest to take control and micromanage the project.

I can't emphasize enough how apparent it is that I'm an outsider. I've lived a rather anonymous life in California. I'm just your normal beachgoer, blending in with every other Barbie. But here, among the bronze-skinned and large-framed Tongans, I'm quite the sight. So, when I come strutting on the boat with my pale white skin, intense green eyes, and a purpose, everyone takes notice. My mind is racing with desire to take control of the messed-up situation. Clearly, the Tongans have existed for thousands of years without outsider help, and now they have me! I can show them how it is done! It is obvious, however, that they see me as entertainment and about as important as a mosquito. This, of course, makes me even more determined.

After speaking my broken Tongan, acting important and demanding, I get nowhere—except behind schedule. After the Tongan men successfully get the boat off of the ferry—without my help—I am relieved, but I am also a bit embarrassed by my behavior. However, I'm pleased because now, I can really take charge of getting the boat into the water. I get behind the wheel of my little brown Toyota pickup, which was shipped over in the 20' x 20' container. The pickup is fitted with a trailer hitch that can connect it to the boat trailer. I've been helping my dad back a boat trailer down into the ocean since I was a little girl. It's my turn now to do it on my own. I proudly back my new boat and trailer down the boat ramp, only to see the trailer fall off the hitch and the boat skid down the ramp toward the sea. Yikes! Is this really happening to me? Thank goodness, the boat stops before crashing into the wall of the ramp.

The Tongan men must not have hooked up the trailer properly. That's the only reason I can figure as to why it fell off the hitch. Idiots! I think. What idiots! I carefully back the truck down and attach the trailer again myself. Now I have an audience of local Tongans watching me even more closely. I'd better get it right this time. I pull the truck part way up the ramp to straighten out, and the trailer falls off again! Shrieks of laughter pierce my ears. I have just elevated myself one notch higher to front and center stage of the O'lavaha experience. Remember? The ferry only comes to town once every other month; it is always an event! The young Tongan boys are rolling on the ground in laughter, pointing and saying: "Pa'alangi!" *Pa'alangi* means "foreigner with white skin." Today, I think it means "OMG! Look it is the stupid Pa'alangi woman." While they are laughing at me, I am getting madder by the minute and feeling like the Tongan men are stupid and incompetent. Do you think I might consider looking at myself? Na!

It turns out the trailer is from New Zealand. Who would have thought that a Kiwi trailer and an American truck hitch are not compatible? Sounds like a bad date on a dating website! My assumptions and lack of research get me in trouble once again. This only compounds the damage done by my ugly judgmental attitude.

I realize that the normal way of launching a boat is not going to work. I'm also aware that every time I try to manage something in my old way, the process is not effective or efficient. Hmmm … change is not easy, even when it's moving in the direction of the life change I want. Now, the tide is too low for launch, which is completely my fault, because I altered the schedule with my micromanagement. I think I'm in a pickle.

I need help. So, I turn to my new friend, Tomasi, the manager of the Moorings Yacht Charter Company. I admire him for his understanding of how to manage people in this country. He organizes six very big local Tongan men to come back at midnight to help me launch the boat at high tide.

"Are you nuts?" I say. "What makes you think they are going to come back at midnight to help me? How much money did you offer them?"

Tomasi smiles and says, "You have a lot to learn, my dear. I told them you would give each one of them a package of cookies. They don't want your money. They'll do it out of the kindness of their hearts and for the benefit their stomachs!"

Midnight comes and passes. The men arrive late, by American standards, on time by Tongan. They launch the boat with their bodies and ropes … by slowly walking it down the ramp in their jeans and bare feet. I stand there in amazement; my thoughts are like a rushing change of tides. I can't believe these men have come to help without being paid, in the middle of the night, no less. And they are very welcoming. Again, I note that a warm smile is worth a thousand words. Then I watch the men problem-solve a difficult situation with ease and a couple of ropes. Life and its problems can be simple or complex; sometimes the choice really starts with our thoughts about a situation, which reminds me of a favorite saying: "If you think you can or think you can't … either way, you are right." The Tongan men see the situation as simple, so it is simple for them.

The men put the boat in the water with ease. They hand me the towline, and I direct them to their packages of *Chips Ahoy*. The things I learn that night provide the beginning of many opportunities for growth and development for me as a leader. What a guppy!

My mind wanders to the obvious right before my eyes. How come the men don't wear their swimming trunks, or even shorts? Their feet must be made of leather! They are not wearing shoes, and the boat ramp is hard on bare feet. Is this the norm—for them to swim in long pants? I, of course, am wearing my one-piece swimsuit underneath my cover-up. Truth be told: I hate swimming in the ocean at night. It is a huge fear of mine. I always feel like shark bait. But in I go. I put the bowline in my mouth, swim my new boat out to a mooring, and tie her off. The Tongan boys happily go home with cookies in hand. I make it back to shore, walk home dripping wet, sleep for a few hours, and awake to the next adventure.

Hours later, full of excitement and anxiety, I run down to the harbor to swim out to my new boat and take her for a spin. As I round the corner, expecting to see the beautiful harbor and the sun shining on my boat, I halt in my tracks. Crisis! The foundation of my future livelihood, *Surface Interval*, is sinking. Half the hull is underwater.

In my head, I replay all my steps from the long night before. I know I put the plug in. Boats built small enough to be put on a trailer and stored on land always have a drain plug. You take it out when you bring the boat out of the water, allowing any excess water to escape. Then you put it in before you place the boat back in the water. It's automatic. If you're a boater, you know to put in the drain plug.

> **POSSIBILITY COACHING TIP:**
>
> *The boat incident provides another example to illustrate why you should be careful with your assumptions when entering any new territory. Even when you think you know your subject matter very well, watch your assumptions, and learn to question yourself.*

I figure the hull must have cracks in it from the ferry ride or that "they" dropped the boat when loading it on the ferry. Remember? I wasn't there to supervise the loading. I know it is someone else's fault and certainly not mine. My lifeguard instincts take over, and I jump in the water to go save my boat, when I realize I need help. I don't have a clue what I will do when I get out there.

I run in a panic, dripping wet, down the dirt road to my only friend, good old Tomasi. I must be no end of entertainment on this sleepy island. I tell him what's going on, in between gulps of air from my exertion.

"Did you put the plugs in the boat?" he asks.

"Of course, I put the plug in."

There is a smile in Tomasi's eyes as he says, "I said plugs . . . as in, plural."

"That's ridiculous. I've never heard of a boat having more than one plug," I respond, holding up my index finger. I know many boaters in the world who are reading this and saying, "Duh, of course a boat has more than one." I'm mad. At myself.

Tomasi hands me a bucket. "Just put in the plugs, bail out the water the old-fashioned way, and then drive the boat around the harbor with the bilge pump running until all the water is gone."

I don't even know if I can start the engine, since I didn't get a good look at it in yesterday's confusion. *Bilge pump? Where is the bilge pump, and how do I turn it on?* I think to myself. But I'm not about to trouble Tomasi any further or become the butt of yet another joke. So I take the bucket and run to the other end of the harbor.

After swimming out to my sinking boat, I discover the engine is a 115hp Yamaha. I hope I can figure this out. My confidence is in the toilet at this point. I turn the key, and I am so happy when the engine starts!

It takes forever to get the water drained. I'm driving the boat around the harbor in a bit of a panic. I must repeatedly leave the helm to run to the back of the boat and bucket out more water. My F.E.A.R. is that now I'm going to crash into something, because I'm not driving the boat when I'm bailing water. By this time, I've developed a huge headache, I'm close to tears, and I feel like the phrase *Stupid Pa'alangi* is tattooed on my forehead. If I can get my business started without sinking something, going to jail, or killing myself, it will be a miracle!

So, guess how many plugs the boat had? Five!

I figure out the bilge pump routine, too. Then I decide to view driving the boat and bailing with a bucket at the same time as creativity. I've never before figured just how important my thinking style would be for effective problem solving or transforming my assumptions. Discover Possibility Thinking vs. living in F.E.A.R. I learned to choose between the two, and you can, too. ∎

POSSIBILITY Coaching Session

When people operate on assumptions without taking time to find the truth, this can lead to a disappointing and uncomfortable outcome. Assumptions and F.E.A.R. easily get in the way of the truth.

As I watched the men on the ferry prepare to take the core of my new livelihood—my little boat—off of the ferry, I was riveted with F.E.A.R. Here is how my mind was working:

> I had it in my head that the men were incompetent. My body was in knots and feeling very stressed because I was convinced, with no evidence whatsoever, that they were going to make a mess of getting my boat off of the ferry. I was filled with anxiety, and I anticipated disaster.

The funny thing about F.E.A.R. is that in the present moment, my physical, mental, and emotional self is experiencing the current event as if the F.E.A.R. is real, as if my worst F.E.A.R. has already happened. Remember, F.E.A.R. stands for:

- False
- Evidence
- Appearing
- Real

There was no real evidence that the workers were going to drop the boat and cause it to splinter into a million pieces. In my mind, that possibility "appeared" real, and my emotions, actions, and behaviors followed suit. I was anxious and felt out of control, which prompted me to act demanding and take control. My behavior was detrimental and demeaning to the workers, who were just helping me out.

If I had chosen instead to get rid of the F.E.A.R. and replace it with Possibility Thinking, here's how it might have looked:

> These Tongan men working on the ferry are so big and strong they could probably lift the little boat off the ferry without the crane. They have been running this ferry boat for years, even though the Pa'alangi call it the *Floating Coffin*. I wonder what I can learn about teamwork by watching them work together. I'm going to keep an open mind to learning a new process.

If I had used Possibility Thinking, my body would not have been tied up in knots, and my demeanor would have been collaborative, rather than combative. My actions would have been to praise and possess an attitude of gratitude, rather than expressing myself as bossy and critical. Of course, a warm smile, instead of a scowl, would have been on my face.

In what situations do you need to change your thoughts from F.E.A.R. to Possibility Thinking? When you find yourself acting bossy, demanding, and controlling, realize that some sort of

F.E.A.R. has its grip on you. As soon as you can, move to a place where you can be alone. Then write the answers to these questions:

- What are the facts about the situation you are in? Write facts only, not emotions. Even though you might be feeling heightened emotions, get clear on just the facts.

- What are you assuming will happen; what feels like the truth to you?

- What is it that has you so scared? Use this phrase as you begin to write your response: I'm afraid that…

- What is the false evidence? What is fact? What is based on your beliefs and fears?

The answers to these questions should help clarify the situation for you. The time it takes to answer the questions should give you the distance you need to make a better decision about what to do next— based on facts and reality—not False Evidence Appearing Real.

— VOGANISM —

When you allow your
F.E.A.R. to overshadow your faith,
your dreams disappear.

Anywhere Is PARADISE . . . It Is Up to You

Every one of us has experienced stress in our lives at one time or another. It cracks me up in America when a medical doctor is evaluating a patient and asking, "Are you under stress?" I laugh and think: *Show me someone who is not under stress, and that person is probably dead!* This story describes how high levels of stress can affect the physical, mental, emotional, and spiritual aspects of our lives.

At the end of the world as we know it, the only things left on the planet will be cockroaches and disposable diapers.

We've all heard this, but I didn't really believe it until I moved to Tonga. The cockroaches there are well on their way to taking over the world. They not only fly, they have a turbo switch that propels them to high speeds. They are huge; they seem to have a wingspan of at least six feet across. They have advanced radar; they dive bomb right for your face with the turbo jets running. And when they hit you, it doesn't faze them; they just bounce off and keep going. If only the military could train them!!

I'll never forget my first night after moving into my Pa'alangi house. It hadn't been lived in for months—by humans, that is. As soon as I opened the front door, the fight began between the cockroaches and me. I figure, since I am paying the rent, they have to go. I open the window to gently swish them out; they invite their cousins in to join us. I kill one with my flip-flop and almost barf. It's just too gross to describe the sound and smell of cockroach guts squirting all over. I reach back into my childhood, remembering the effectiveness of an old glass jar and a piece of cardboard I plan to sneak up and put the glass jar over a cockroach while slipping the cardboard under the glass. Then I will walk outside to the jungle and toss it as far away as possible and race to beat the cockroaches back inside the house. I manage this a few times, then realize it is futile. Southern California is the sissy-la-la land for bugs and spiders. I was one of those silly people who grew up not having a clue what a real spider looked like, except for a tarantula, the one a geeky boy brought to school. Okay, that was the ugliest and the biggest spider I'd ever seen until Tonga. Now 5mm spiders are the daddy long-legs of Tonga—innocuous. I'm once again the talk of the town because I hire a Tongan to make screens for every window. After getting the screens, I manage to get rid of most of the cockroaches, their cousins, the centipedes, and a few other living creatures. Things are looking up in the Animal House. The fruit bats stay outside, as do the pigs, goats, chickens, the mangy dogs, and of course the built-in alarm clock . . . the local rooster.

The bathroom is outside in the jungle. It's made out of cement with a tin roof and wooden door. No bathtub, shower or hot water, but I'm feeling very fortunate to have a real sit-down and flushing toilet. Though the door is open about two feet on the bottom and the top, it still provides a bit of privacy. From what? I'm not sure yet. Maybe the pigs?

And then I see it. Up in the back corner where the ceiling meets the wall, just above the toilet, is the comfortable home of Mr. and Mrs. Coconut Spider, larger versions of the ugly tarantula of my childhood.

From that point forward, each time I go into the hut to do my business, I refuse to sit on the toilet for fear one of coconut spiders will drop from the ceiling into my thick head of hair, which would make a great nest. I'm convinced I will not be able to get up fast enough to move out of the way. It is TMI (too much information) to tell you how I conducted business, other than to say that I never took my eyes off of the spider couple.

Coconut spiders are plentiful in Tonga, and they decided to start showing up inside the main house, as well. These guys are big, hairy, and ugly. They have two fangs that look like they could open a can of soup without any trouble. They can stay upside down on the ceiling without moving forever. Then, all of a sudden, they move like lightning—extra large tarantulas with jet propulsion!

Oh my, how am I going to get rid of them? I try to spray them with hairspray and every other spray product I can get my hands on. They just laugh. Of course, the local store does not carry bug spray; the Tongans just live with these spiders as though they're pets. But I can't do that. It's just so unnerving to have them in the house. I can't get myself to just hang out with them. I tire of throwing things at them; I miss 99 percent of the time. (One time, I nail one, and when it hits the ground and dies, it seems to shrink to a quarter of its size.)

It takes my creative juices a while to kick in on this adventure, but finally, I get smart. I buy a house broom that's long enough to swing like a baseball bat. I hit the spiders on the ceiling and then sweep out their half-dead, one-quarter bodies. My batting average gets pretty good throughout the years.

. . . .

Beginning the second week of my stay in my new home, I'm almost adept at turning the light switch up for down and down for up. Or is that on for off and off for on? And I've created an ingenious way to pee in the middle of the night without the necessity of going outside in the pitch-black jungle, down two flights of uneven stairs, and into the coconut spiders' little hut home. On one night, as midnight quickly approaches, I can't sleep, so I read—*A Pirate Looks at 50* by Jimmy Buffett. Since I am still twenty years away from fifty, I'm thinking it might be humorous or at least provide a glimpse into my future. The noises outside are really weird

on this particular night. In fact, I find them very scary and annoying. I think someone might be walking outside my bedroom window. The more I listen, the more I hear what I think is each footstep nearing my window. I turn off all the lights in the house and go to the bedroom window to throw open the curtain. I see nothing. No one is there, and the noise mysteriously stops. I turn on the light, get back into bed, and it starts again. This time, I lie there and just listen. I hear the sound of leaves crackling underfoot, as if someone is shuffling along the exterior of my bedroom wall. I have this horrible vision of someone standing on tiptoes, trying to get a peek into the new Pa'alangi's house. So many emotions run through my head, and of course I have a two-tank dive scheduled in the morning. I need some sleep. The more I lie there, the madder I get. I've had it. I get up, get out my Louisville Slugger open the back door, and stay close to the house as I head for the back, where my bedroom window is, so I can surprise the culprit.

To my surprise, I look straight ahead, cocked and ready to swing, and see nothing! Except a big pig that stares me down from about twenty feet away. I scream; it snorts. We run in opposite directions. I get back in bed, half-laughing, half-crying, and wondering what happened to the logical brain I used to own. It clearly left me. What was I thinking?

I pick up the book, take a deep breath, relax in the sound of silence, and let Jimmy Buffett take me away. It's an especially hot night, as it's summer. The humidity is so thick that the blades on my fan even find it hard to move. My mosquito net is draped over my bed, and I finally feel secure and as if I might drift off to la-la land soon.

I feel a kind of tingle or tickle on my ankle and figure; I think it's the sheet or some nerve in my body. I ignore it. The feeling grows stronger, and then I feel it run from my ankle up the outside of my leg and across the top of my left thigh. Now, I know this is not a nerve.

I kick off the sheet in a quick contortionist fashion. It is a giant centipede! It's big and ugly, a 12-inch-long monster with huge pincers at the head. On top of all that, it's fast! Without enough time to scream, I need every bit of oxygen to think quickly. Centipedes are highly poisonous creatures in these parts. The Tongan centipedes are so bad that they can kill a cat, not to mention doing some serious damage to a human. I grab the hardcover book and take a swat at the centipede. I miss. The giant bug bounces from the bed into the air and back to the bed, changing direction. It's coming straight at me! I jump out of bed and it runs down the side of the bed frame. I take a hard swing and knock the centipede against the side of the wooden bed. That move cuts it in half, but both halves keep moving. I feel like I'm in a science fiction movie by this time. I use the book to squish both halves. They stink to high heaven. So gross!

Thank goodness, Jimmy Buffett has come to my rescue! ■

POSSIBILITY Coaching Session

Isn't it amazing what stress can do to you physically, mentally, emotionally, and spiritually? You can become a laser beam of logic, or your logical brain can fly out the window! How can you encourage your brain to create productive—not paralyzing—images and give you the power for quick thinking and emergency problem-solving?

How often do you operate in crisis mode? Guess what your body is going through? The same chemical releases that I was going through that gave me quick energy and a sharp mind, even through my exhaustion. For emergency, yes! Feeling that way on a regular basis? No. The chemicals released in the body at a high level of continual stress are very harmful over long periods of time.

I know what you are saying: "I'm not like that; I don't have centipedes running up my leg." But you might not realize that you are experiencing a constant level of stress because everybody's levels of stress is unique and individual.

Rate yourself on a scale of 1 to 10, with 10 being the highest in stress:

| **1** | **5** | **10** |
| Low Stress | Medium Stress | High Stress |

Where do you operate most of the time? Use a 30-day cycle as an example. Think of the prior 30 days, and average them. Where does that put you on the scale?

Next, ask three other people who know you well to use the same rating scale to determine their impressions of your stress level. Where do they think you operate most of the time on the stress scale? How big is the gap between how you scored yourself and how others scored you?

If you really want to learn about yourself, ask people you trust to be open and honest with you. Ask them to describe behaviors you exhibit that show them you are stressed. I guarantee that you will learn something new about yourself.

If I had continued to be stressed out and focused on all the gross bugs, no hot water, and no inside toilet, I would have been at a 10 on my stress scale all the time! I would have missed the paradise I was living in. Staying focused on everything that is NOT paradise in your life can leave you living in a tangled jungle of fear and disappointment. Take inventory of your stress level, and ask yourself this question:

• What has my focus? Why?

I can relate this question to my experiences in scuba diving. Never stop breathing is key when you dive. I was well versed in the concept and very comfortable underwater. What I didn't realize was just how important the concept was out of the water.

When many of us become stressed, we stop breathing correctly, which can interfere with how we handle stress and how we run our businesses. One way to get back on track is through a technique I call the Two-Minute Wonder. When life as a leader becomes overwhelming, stop and try this technique that I learned from the owner of the Tongan Beach Resort, Dieter Dyck. It might seem simple, but it works.

This exercise is about using your breath to turn your reactions into responses. I know what you are thinking. I have heard all this "breathing stuff" before, blah, blah, blah. That is exactly the way you will continue to show up for life—blah, blah, blah—unless you choose at this very moment to do it differently. I'm not saying you must do the Two-Minute Wonder—or any other solution. I am asking that you make a conscious decision to just be "open" and watch for possibilities. There is not one person on this Earth who lacks the room to be better in personal or business life in one way or another.

Concentrate on breathing out and letting go of the stress and then inhaling health, success, and peace. People actually lower their blood pressure and heart rate with this technique. I figured that if it worked for the high-energy, constantly stressed German resort owner named Dieter, it had to work for me.

POSSIBILITY COACHING TIP:

Find a place to be alone, even if it is the office restroom, and take some deep breaths. When breathing in, breathe in through your nose with a long and steady breath. Visualize all the good things that represent health to you. Inhale them on your long breath in.

Exhale in the same fashion, long and steady exhale, blowing out through your mouth. Visualize all the stress in your body, and see it being released when you exhale.

Breathe in through your nose three times, and visualize health the first time, success the second time, and peace the third time.

Each time you exhale, push your long steady breath through your mouth, and concentrate on the release of stress each time. Sometimes, keeping it simple is the best for me. Inhale Health, Exhale Stress.

The first time I did this, it was amazing. After the Two-Minute Wonder, my brain was clearer, and I was able to make better business decisions. I could respond thoughtfully, instead of reacting instantly, based on emotion.

The brain is the only organ we have that can question itself. Once we learn just a little bit about the brain, it will help us understand why we feel and think the way we do—and what happens with our interactions. When we repeat a behavior in the same way over and over again, this creates a groove in the brain, kind of like a groove that a worm would eat through an apple. It takes the brain time to stop going down the well-traveled path and move over to a new path it is still developing.

Visualize walking through a lush, dark, deep green forest with one clear and well-traveled path. Now, go off the path and venture out into the forest to create a new path. What feelings come up for you? Often, fear comes up for people when they really get down to their deepest thoughts. Trying something new and creating a new path that you want to use takes determination, creativity, and the right tools. Also, it takes courage to walk through your fears as you travel into the abyss of the unknown. Now, you can see why it is so easy to run back to the well-traveled comfortable path in the forest you know so well. Even if you know the path is longer and not the most efficient route, at least you are honest with yourself about it.

> ### VOGANISM
>
> *All* possibility in life begins in the same place - your thoughts. Discover new ways of thinking, discover possibility.

Like me, I'm sure you've heard people say, "That is just the way I am!" Or, perhaps you've heard them say, "We have always done it that way in this company." In working with companies, especially family-run companies, we help them to apply Possibility Thinking instead of stuck-in-a-rut thinking. Additionally, we use the appropriate tools to help better understand personalities and behaviors.

Remember, anywhere can be paradise. It is up to you to see it that way.

LESSON 6

Where's Da MAN?

Have you ever reacted to a situation and not been happy with how you responded, or the results? Of course, you have; we all have done this more times than we care to admit. This story is about learning the difference between reacting and responding. When we react to something, we usually do it in the heat of the moment, before we can separate our emotion from our action. Anger is often the fuel, and we say or do things we regret. When we respond, though, we take a moment to evaluate the situation and determine the best course of action. We acknowledge the emotion and choose to not let the emotion be the driver, but to let rational thinking steer what we do next.

The first step in shifting from reacting to responding is to become aware of your personal cues when anger or emotion is exercising its hold on you. Some people flush or feel hot. Others find that the heart races, or the stomach does a flip-flop. There are many indicators. What are yours? The next step is figuring out what you need to do to get control of yourself. How can you get away from the heated emotion of needing to be in control—which is reacting—and move toward making a choice—which is responding? Take a deep breath; count to ten. Then step out of the room. Learning to respond, rather than react, is similar to this exercise—a learned skill. Frequently, in a coaching session with a leader, we will review a situation and find out that the emotion attached to the situation sometimes is just a trigger from an earlier life experience, that it really has nothing to do with the exact situation at hand. An epiphany is always hindsight with 20/20 vision. Anyone can learn the skill, respond versus react, at any age.

It is one of my personal beliefs that all of us are in control of our emotions and responses. We have the choice, once we understand how and why we do what we do. Even though you have been doing something the same way for many years, old dogs can learn new tricks.

As my dad used to say to me when I was growing up: "You just have to get your 'want-to' fixed."

. . . .

Building the foundation of my business starts now—in a very literal sense. I must pour two cement slabs for the dive shop and compressor room. I'm a woman on a mission when I walk into the only store in town, Fata Fata Mafana. In this store, we buy bread, motor oil, nails, and half-frozen chickens. I want to get this slab done, so I can get in the water and start diving. Every time I drive between islands or get high enough to see the ocean sparkling over the reef, I feel an incredible urge to forget about all the work ahead of me and just dive in the water. But instead, here I am, walking out of Fata Fata Mafana, empty-handed. The store owners told me I have to see the Minister of Works for what I need – cement, rebar, and other materials for the foundation. Once again, I tell myself: *Things just work a little differently here. I need to go with the flow.*

Most Tongans speak English, but the farther you get from the bigger islands, the less that is true. I bound into the Minister's office, which resembles a primitive DMV, wearing a wide smile. I do a little happy wave and try my best to hurdle the language barrier by speaking through the window: "Build dive shop. Need cement, rebar, coral—the crushed kind." I hand him my list of supplies.

He doesn't look at the list. Or at me. It's like I'm invisible.

I look behind me. Nothing. As I look back to the Minister, it seems he's still focused on the door. I look again. Still nothing there.

Okay . . .

And we are waiting for . . . what? My smile caves. What the heck is going on?

"Where's da man?" he says.

"Uh," I start speaking louder and making hand motions to make my point. "Build dive shop on Utungake Island with Dieter. You know? German. And wife, Senikau." Senikau is a Tongan native.

"No man; no buy," he says matter-of-factly, slamming his palm on the counter.

There is a man: Dieter.

"Me. Dieter. Build. Utungake." I explain with more hand motions resembling hammering and sawing.

"No man; no buy."

"Dieter. You know Dieter? German?" My volume increases even more. Like that's going to make him understand.

"No man; no buy."

Are you kidding me? I can see he won't be listening today, unless I can magically sprout a beard and talk a few octaves deeper. How can we talk when he won't even look at me? I exit the building with my shoulders slack, gazing at my feet as I kick through the sandy road. Superman isn't due for more than a month. *No* is not okay. I really hate the word *No!*

I head up the hill from Neiafu Harbor to my little house. My slow shuffle turns into a stomp on the dirt road. Chickens and pigs scatter out of my path. My fists are balled, and tears flow. As I walk by, I turn my head away from the two men speaking on the outside phones at Telecom. The long bank of phones is the only place on the island to talk, as most houses don't have phones. My heart wants to call Superman, and the bank account says, *No!* My house is lonely, save for the ever-present Mr. Cockroach and Mrs. Coconut Spider. All the while, I'm muttering aloud:

"You have got to be f-ing kidding me! Tell me I did not just hear him say I cannot buy stuff because I do not have a man to buy it for me." By this time, I'm beginning to realize the whole system is against a woman starting a business on her own. I'm not mad at the Minister; it's the system I'm fighting.

I walk inside, slamming the door. The house seems to agree with my feelings and creaks back in complaint. Solidarity, at last.

"Arrrrgh!"

I don't need commiseration. I need action. I stomp right back outside and pace.

"Where am I?" I yell up at the spider hanging on her web between the birds of paradise flowers. "Is this place for real?"

Mrs. Spider shows about the same interest as the man at the counter.

"F-ing unbelievable!" I spit and kick sand some more. I had no clue Tonga was going to be this prejudiced against women. Discrimination in its finest form. I have money and want to buy a product. They won't do business with me just because I am a woman! I have never been a huge women's libber, but I'm about to become one. Still, getting angry and acting demanding and micromanaging haven't worked for me so far. *There must be a way around this stupid mess, I say to myself. I have come this far, and I'm not going to let this stop me.*

The adrenaline slow-drips out of me through my fingertips, which hang loosely toward the ground. My thoughts transition: *How am I gonna' change this 'tude?*

The change has to start with me first.

Ahhhh . . . a challenge. Now, that is a fun way to look at it.

I know! Dietmar will be Da Man. Dietmar is twelve years my junior and Dieter's only son. He will be my man for the day. I grab him from the Tongan Beach Resort and half drag him back to the Minister of Works with my supply list, coaching him all the way there: "Say *yes* to everything he asks," I tell him, waving my trusty list. Upon entering the cinderblock building, my power position shifts from ordering Dietmar around to hiding a bit behind the "boy." It's not that the Minister is mean; he's just so big and imposing that I naturally shy away. Plus, recent events hint this might not go too well. Dietmar's body language spells t-r-a-p-p-e-d. Now I must burden him by asking him to associate with me—the crazy American woman! He's gotta be strategic about helping me—just enough to get my business off the ground, because it adds to the resort's offerings, but not so much as to alienate his current status at the Tongan Beach Resort and among local friends.

I work up the courage and step forward to hand the Minister my list. He waves it away like he would a buzzing, biting gnat. Instead of railing at the injustice of it all, I bite my bottom lip to keep it zipped. Is that blood I taste? The Minister's gaze isn't on the door this time. He's staring at my dutiful new man. He starts down the checklist of items.

Dietmar nods, saying "'io," which is the Tongan word for *yes.*

"'io."

All the way down the list: "'io."

"'io." Very dutiful, indeed. I owe Dietmar, big time.

I sigh with relief. My dive shop will have its foundation—a plain, solid hunk of concrete upon which I will build my dream. I nod in deference, whispering my thanks, "Malo 'aupito."

When I look up, the mighty Minister and I lock eyes. He turns away. ■

POSSIBILITY Coaching Session

Sometimes, as leaders, we get blocked by so many barriers within a "system" that we think we can't do anything to change it. We make it even more difficult by reacting instead of responding. It's important to let go of assumptions about how things "should" be. Changing the word *should* to *could* when you speak can dramatically change your outcomes. The word *should* is stubborn and pedantic. The word *could* opens the mind to allow Possibility Thinking.

Often, the phrase *but I really don't want to* is attached to a *should*. I should (but I really don't want to) write down my goals. Listen to the same thought phrased this way: *I could write down my goals*. The word 'could' leaves space for opportunity and gets the Possibility Thinking juices flowing. Options abound if we open up our belief systems and engage in learning new ways to respond.

Once you become aware that you really are in control of your own outcome, then you can look at the difference between reaction and response. Most of the time, humans are reactionary creatures. Reacting means you act based on emotions before you give yourself time to respond logically and rationally. When you choose to respond, you could pause, even for half a second, just long enough to remember that you are in charge of how you choose to respond to a situation. That half of a second is very powerful.

If you were sitting in front of me now, I would ask you to:

- Remember a time when you reacted and were not happy with yourself afterward.

- Think of a situation with an employee, a customer, even a child.

- See if you can pinpoint the symptoms or cues that your body gave just before you reacted. Can you think of any?

If you are having a hard time understanding what the heck your body does, don't feel bad; you are not alone on this journey.

Self-awareness is about noticing the cues your body will give you before you speak. Understanding yourself as a leader is the first step to being proficient at responding instead of reacting. Some people feel their bodies get hot; some people turn red or get shaky hands or sweaty palms.

Be mindful of yourself, and take notice. Awareness alone can create powerful change.

VOGANISM

Your personal beliefs will color the

canvas of your world.

LESSON 7

Latitudes and ATTITUDES

Culture, strong or weak, is present in all countries, families, and corporations. A strong culture is witnessed when a group of people internalize and live their actions in alignment with the values of a company. Families with strong values make good decisions because they take into consideration what will be best for the group, not just one person. A weak culture in business or family is indicated when there is little representation of values, and control is exercised with strong attention to rules and regulations. Notice in this story how an internal view of culture can dramatically change an external attitude.

. . . .

In the Hawaiian language, there's a name for locals: *kama'aina*. Kama'aina get special airfare, discounts at tourist attractions, and license to call foreigners *haole*. Tonga is another Polynesian country with a similar practice. Foreigners are christened *Pa'alangi* upon arrival, and never locals shall they be.

Today I visit the bank. I pull on a clean blue Dolphin Pacific Diving polo shirt and long-to-the-knee shorts. I decide I'd better open up a bank account and stop using cash, which is called *pa'angas*. I'm not the bookkeeper in the relationship, and Superman will want a detailed description of the accounting when he gets here.

The bank feels overly civilized, compared to all the open-air buildings in town. It's closed to the outside by real windows and doors and a cement sidewalk. There are no paved roads, stop signs, or stoplights in Vava'u. A sidewalk is really uptown. I'm accustomed to hearing the wind in the palms and having the humidity follow me inside. The hum of air conditioning sounds completely alien as I enter.

A woman wearing a three-quarter-sleeve shirt with a tapa cloth design around the cuffs, a traditional ta'avala around her waist to show respect, and a long ivory-colored skirt greets me at the door. She's also wearing a plumeria flower in her long black hair, which is done up in a bun. Her nametag reads *Kafu'atu* in gold letters.

"Can I help you?"

"Yes, I'm here to open a bank account."

She nods understandingly and motions for me to sit at the reception desk. I see the bank manager sitting behind the bank counter, jovially visiting with a man I recognize as a legendary local German Pa'alangi fisherman. I learned of him while engrossed in one of Heintz's fishing tales at The Paradise Hotel bar a few weeks earlier. His nickname is The Lone Ranger. It doesn't matter that he fishes alone; I believed every word. The bank manager is equally rapt and not in any rush to make his way to me.

I'm running my thumb and forefinger back and forth along my shirt collar and staring at the piece of paper folded to hold up one leg of the desk, when the manager suddenly appears right next to me.

"Hello, Betty!" he booms, holding out his hand. He knew my name and used it? With a Tongan accent, my name—Patty—comes out sounding like *Beh-Tea*, emphasis on the *Tea*.

I stand to shake his hand. "So, my reputation precedes me?"

"No, no. Dieter was in this morning and told me you'd be in." Good 'ole Dieter, looking out for me. Dieter is the German owner of the Tongan Beach Resort. My dive shop will be located on resort property. Superman nailed down all the business details with Dieter during the last days of our honeymoon. He's also friends with Tomasi, but of a whole different type. He's very serious and not as approachable with his tough German exterior; he's a teddy bear underneath, but we won't blow his cover.

The manager motions for me to sit back down and scoots himself in behind the desk.

"So," he says. "How can I help you?"

"I'd like to open a business checking account, please," I say proudly.

He replies, "Where's da man—your husband—Betty?"

I just about fall out of my chair.

I stare at him like a deer in the headlights, you know, one of those out-of-body experiences when you can't believe something is happening for real.

"My husband will be here next week," I say, with my hands crossed in my lap.

"That will be just fine." He rustles through his desk drawer and pulls out a notepad without making eye contact. "We will wait until he arrives."

Nothing to do but stand, turn, and walk out before the steam emerges from my ears and nostrils! My inner voice is ranting and raving. You've got to be kidding me. Not again!

Okay. I can kind of get it about the Minister of Works and all the building materials. After all, that could be thought of as traditional guy stuff. But the bank? Gimme a break! I'm going to give you money—and you won't take it because I am female? Arrrrghh!

Later that evening at my little home above the harbor, I'm sipping my favorite vintage of boxed Australian wine and watching the sun set over the verdant green islands. Reflecting on the day, I realize I am viewing the bank situation through my narrow-minded American standards. Thinking about the differences between the Tongan culture and the culture I was reared in makes me realize I'm not looking at or taking into consideration their culture at all. The blinders near my eyes are wide and thick. Just maybe, the bank situation doesn't have anything to do with being a woman? Maybe it has to do with family or just two partners being present in a business transaction? Wine can be very therapeutic.

As I remove the blinders and see the beauty of the Tongan culture, my attitude starts to change. ■

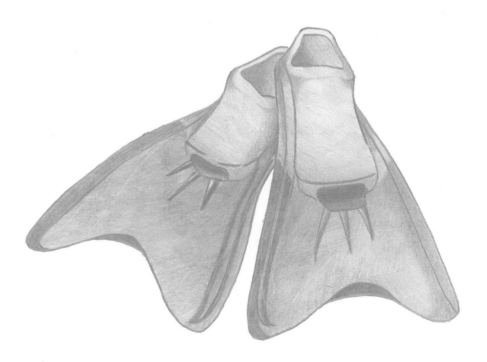

POSSIBILITY Coaching Session

As I am an executive business leader, some corporations have hired me to change the culture to "make it better." There are benefits to stepping back to watch and learn from the culture already in existence. It's hard to make something better, or even worse for that matter, if you don't know what it stands for today.

Take a step back see if you can take off your own blinders and view your culture—family and business—as an outsider. What does your culture stand for in your business and/or family? How do values play a part in your culture? Ask people within and outside of your company how they would describe your culture and the values of the company. Compare your description to theirs, and see what you can learn. It will probably amaze you.

VOGANISM

History bears the fruits of your culture; judgments will kill your future

---

Again, it is really important to understand where you, your family, and your company stand right now—before you have an opportunity to change the culture. Even if you have never actually articulated the culture of your company, you will find that it has a life of its own and will develop and morph all by itself. The troops in a company are usually rather good at stating what the "unsaid" culture of a company expresses.

Lights, Camera . . . NO Action

You are all set, ready to go, and . . . nothing. What went wrong? Why is your well-thought-out plan not working? What is the flaw in the system? Frustration sets in quickly—and then defeat. This lesson is about cultural and language differences. So many times, I know what my intention is when I am delivering a message or asking a question, but my receiver hears what I have to say in a different way—due to cultural differences or simply choice of words. Everyone in this story speaks English, but watch what happens when we interpret word meaning differently.

. . . .

The sand sits in a pile by the cement mixer. Before I pick up the shovel again, I look toward the heavens and whisper a wish that all will go well.

The Tongan Beach Resort spreads out quietly behind my bustling construction site. Again, I'm trying to get this done quickly, so as not to disrupt Dieter's business or disturb his guests too much. I've plotted out two square pads on the sandy ground. They are far enough from the wharf to be safe in a storm surge. Since we're in the Port of Refuge Harbor, I'm relatively confident we would have minimal storm damage during cyclone season. I hire a helper.

Boatbuilding is his profession, but he's now living on his sailboat and sailing around the world. He is my handyman helper for the week. I figure if he can build a boat, he can surely build a dive shop. I think half the reason I hired him was because I liked the name of his boat, the *Southern Cross*. Now, I know what you're thinking: *That's a sound management decision. Good system for hiring employees!* Sometimes, I just trust my gut, and it all works out. Does that ever happen to you?

First, I fire up the generator, so we can plug in the cement mixer and get started. I plug the thick utility cord into the generator and drag the other end to the faded red mixer. I plug it into the mixer, expecting a roaring creaking sound as it spins to life. Instead . . . nothing. It's completely dead.

We check the wiring. The boatbuilder takes the mixer halfway apart. Two hours later, we're still no better off, just hotter. The Minister from the village comes by to check on us, and he even prays over the thing.

I've had it. I jump in the truck and drive into town to find Isaiah, my landlord and the owner of the cement mixer.

I find his truck parked at Fata Fata Mafana, long name for the only store in town.

"Isaiah!" I flag him down as he's getting back into his truck with a grocery bag full of nails, motor oil, and frozen sipi, some sort of weird looking meat.

He's sitting on the bench seat of his truck, facing me, with his legs hanging out. I put my left hand on the doorframe, almost caging him in while I run down the whole long morning. I'm careful to include all the mechanical details of fixes we tried. He nods the whole time and squints at the sun behind me.

I finish with, "So do you know what could be wrong? Can you fix it?"

"Betty," he says. "When you asked to borrow it, you did not ask if it worked. I know it no work."

He smiles, showing bright white teeth from ear to ear. I know by now he's not being malicious. It just never occurred to him. He was being generous by giving me what I asked for: the cement mixer. Since I didn't ask if it worked, he assumed I didn't need it to work.

I smack myself in the head and think: *This must be a joke, right?* I've learned to keep my thoughts to myself. No joke. Isaiah is a really nice man without a mean bone in his body. The only thing my brain can come up with at that moment is that this must be a case of American common sense having a different definition than Tongan common sense. He looks at me with his big brown eyes and says, "Sorry, Betty," and drives off. For all I know, Isaiah could have thought I wanted to use the dead cement mixer as a flowerpot for decoration.

Still, my body sags in defeat. I slink back to the truck and slowly drive back to the worksite. Now what? How am I going to build a foundation without the tools? Just giving up is not an option I want to accept. In the midst of feeling defeat, I will persevere and find a way to make it happen!

I can see Isaiah following me. It is obvious he feels bad. When we park at the site, he gets right to work. He pulls a large sheet of plywood and some hand trowels out of his truck bed. I get a lesson in mixing cement by hand.

My team frames up the foundation, places the rebar, and pours the hand-mixed cement. The blisters on my hand and wrist scream in pain, not to mention the issue of my lower-back agony after bending over to mix and shovel in and spread the cement.

If we are going to run short on anything, it would be nice to find it is a product actually stocked in town. I don't want to hear: "Of course we do not have that; that is not The Tongan Way." I can see this will become a very familiar statement.

69

We run out of sand. "Oh, big deal. There's a beach full of it," I say to the boys. The boatbuilder and the Tongan boy, Moses, split a gut laughing at me. I start by laughing, too, though I'm not sure why.

The boys explain: "Clean sand. Our cement slabs need clean sand."

"The beach looks clean enough to me," I say.

They explain what would happen to the slab if we were to use the sand with salt in it. The foundation would rust, crack, and fall apart where the bolts are inserted. I flash on a company back home that had the wrong people working in it, and they always seemed to be cracking and falling apart. They had a weak foundation because they didn't use the right material, the right people; they had a few rusty spots that caused the problems. I guess building a structure in the tropics is not so different from building a strong company or corporation.

At this point, Dieter hears the commotion and heads over to help. "You can get clean sand from the church." He points over his shoulder and up the hill behind him.

"What? Has it been blessed?" I'm sweating.

I get a deep, hearty laugh in reply. From all of them. In fact, they can't stop laughing as they turn away to head back to the resort.

I drop my shovel. Off I go to church.

As I approach the construction site for the new church, I spot the church minister inspecting the progress, wearing his lava lava skirt and ta'avala. All men wear this formal attire to church and royal gatherings. He's framed by a massive pile of sand and cinderblock. He turns as I approach. Every time I meet someone new, I have the feeling the person has already "met" me through the village stories. So, I wave without introduction.

"I hear you have clean sand?" I gesture toward the pile.

"Yes," he nods. "Clean. We washed it to build the new church."

We stand together, arms crossed, and observe the mound like it's an animal at the zoo.

After a moment, he asks, "Will you be coming to Mass?"

"I had a feeling you'd say that." The following Sunday, I experience true Tongan devotion. The church doesn't sing in front of the congregation, as in so many American churches. Instead, the choir is made up of the whole congregation. Congregants don't sit with their families; they sit where their voices sound best. The entire church sings a cappella, and the sound is loud, bold, and held together by all the voices singing from thousands of years earlier. The magnificence hits me with a flourish of goose bumps.

My new friend, the minister, donates clean sand to my cause. What goes around comes around; I happily make a financial donation to the church. We do it all again the following day, so I can pour the slab for the compressor room, once again with holy sand. ∎

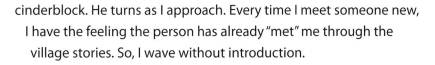

POSSIBILITY Coaching Session

We are sitting in my office overlooking the blue Pacific, and I ask you this question: "What do your employees or co-workers need to hear from you?" You look at me with a blank stare. So often, we are so busy telling everyone what we think they need to hear, and we say it over and over and over again and get frustrated when "they just don't get it!"

I ask again, "What do your employees or co-workers want to hear from you?" That question can be answered if we look at it from a couple of different angles. Consider first that an old saying is still useful and true: "Before you criticize a man, walk a mile in his moccasins." It is important for you to think and feel like the people you are managing— in order to really know what they need and want from you to be the best employees they can be. Everybody needs and wants to know the direction of the company. Yes, this is true. How many ways are there to describe that? Is there more than just your way, which reflects what is important to you? Yes, even though sometimes it doesn't seem that way. The secret is to really understand how your message will best be received, not how well you can tell it. This is the key to success in communication.

Another light to shine on the question relates to culture. "What are the cultural norms in your company?" Many cultural norms are unwritten and unspoken, but they are very much present. Take them into consideration, too.

Look at the cultural differences that were evident when I asked to use the cement mixer. It did not make Isaiah or me right or wrong in the approach to each other, just different. Isaiah didn't care what I wanted to use the mixer for and didn't see the need to quiz me about it. He assumed I knew it didn't work, while I assumed it did work. In Tonga, a Kingdom far from many suppliers, many items are used for a variety of purposes not originally intended, and that is a common cultural thread within the Kingdom. That is why a garden hose was once cut up and used as a hose replacement in the engine of my truck, which represents resourcefulness in a place where replacement parts are not always immediately available.

VOGANISM

Common sense is often our greatest advisor.

Let's take a look at a fifty-year-old employer giving instructions to a new twenty-year-old employee. There is a 30-year generation gap here, and the intention of the 50-year-old may not be heard by the twenty-year-old. Perhaps the fifty-year-old was reared in a business culture where you took the bull by the horns and figured things out on your own. Perhaps the twenty-year-old has been reared to check back with every step of the instruction to make sure she is still aligned, as priorities can change so quickly. Is one way right and the other wrong? No, the two ways are just different.

So, take inventory of yourself to see how you can embrace cultural differences. Continue to craft your message so that everyone can hear it.

KABOOM!

How many times have you heard comments such as: "That's not my job! There is nothing I can do about that!" Or perhaps you've heard my all-time favorite: "I can't . . . it's our company policy!"

This story relates to finding solutions to problems you have not previously encountered. Discovering the powerful relationship among determination, persistence, and patience—and discovering Possibility Thinking—can be life-changing for anyone.

. . . .

The compressor room houses the loud engine I brought with me to fill the scuba tanks with air. I know the power grid in Tonga is 220 volts, not 110 volts. When I had the compressor built back in the States, I had the motor changed to 220 volts. I drew a schematic with the help of the compressor company, since I knew I would be setting up the compressor myself. I tried to anticipate my needs in Tonga before my move, but I am neither an engineer, nor an electrician.

It's almost sunset when we start up the compressor for the first time. The dive shop sits behind the Tongan Beach Resort's twelve rooms. The sun sets over calm seas, and the lights come on in the village . . . until the power surge from my compressor blows out every light and fries itself. KABOOM! Hmm . . . I feel a surge of unpopularity coming my way.

I go straight to the Power Board and ask for the top guy. This strategy has worked for me in the past back home, so I'm sure it will work for me now. I meet Pal'e One Tooth, as he's known about town for his distinctive feature: one big tooth in front, the majority of the others missing. He agrees to accompany me back to the worksite. With his broken English and one tooth accent, it is a long truck ride back to the resort. Even though I can't understand him well, Pal'e and I become quick friends. A great deal of communication can happen through head nods, smiles, and laughter. I'm sure he's going to get my compressor running smoothly right away, after he gets power back to the resort and village. That only took a few hours. Now, it's my turn.

We drive back down to the resort, hop out of the car with me resembling the impatient hare and Pal'e resembling the steadfast turtle. He lumbers over to the compressor to take a look. He checks it out from one angle, then another. I'm bouncing around frantically in stark relief to his steady stare. I look around him, trying to see what he sees.

Pal'e leaves me there with the blown up engine and wanders up towards the village. Huh? I want to scream at him and say, "What the hell do we do now?" But I've discovered over and over and over again the importance of being patient and showing respect, so I say nothing. I think to myself, *Maybe if I just chill and let him do it "The Tongan Way," it will all work out*. That lasts all of about thirty seconds. "The Tongan Way" is just not fast enough for me. I can't sit here without doing anything.

So, what do I do first? I look over the engine as if I am going to figure it out. Remember, I am accustomed to having the answer and looking smart. Then it occurs to me: I might look stupid, but I don't have to act stupid. I can write down all the steps we took to blow up the compressor, and maybe that will help get it fixed. This could be especially helpful since Pal'e wasn't here when I pushed the final button and blew it up.

Pal'e comes back down the hill and waves at me to get the truck and take him back to town. Off we go on the bumpy, dusty, dirty pothole-filled road back to town. My truck never gets out of second gear; too bad I can't sell third and fourth gear and make some money. Pal'e is, of course, silent.

I can't stand it anymore. "So, what do you think?"

He says, "Compressor blow up, go boom, not free phase."

I refuse to comment and ask another question. "Can we fix it?"

I get the blank stare.

I rephrase it. "Make better; make go. You know . . . " I pucker my lips and make blowing sounds. Then I start to laugh, and so does Pal'e.

I get him back to town and drop him off. "I'll come talk tomorrow," I explain. I've had as much as I can take for one day in trying to communicate. Geez . . . if I could speak better Tongan, that would make a huge difference in my life—and probably in how I'm treated here.

At night, I go see Julia and John-Boy from Sailing Safari because John-Boy used to be an electrician when he lived in New Zealand. We call it his "previous life," meaning life before Tonga. I pull out my notepad and read him each step that led to the compressor disaster.

He looks at me and rolls his eyes. Julia hands me a beer. "I don't have a clue what you just said. Sit down, relax and I'll come look at it tomorrow."

"But, but, but, but . . . " I mutter.

"No *buts*, girl. When are you going to learn?"

I must say that the Tongan beer tasted really good.

The next day, John-Boy informed me how lucky I'd been. "It should have been designed to be three phase, not one phase, and a few other things are wrong, but it's fixable."

All I care about is that last word—fixable.

"Can you fix it, John-Boy?" I ask, full of hope.

"Yes." Music to my ears. We scavenge parts from his boat, the town store, the dive shop, and the Power Board, thanks to Pal'e. I think Pal'e ended up happy he didn't have to deal with me anymore. And I learned that screwing up is not a reason to give up. By evening, we were sitting in The Sand Bar at The Tongan Beach Resort, having a beer and celebrating as I joyfully ran back and forth filling tanks.

Each time I make mistakes and find myself in a precarious position, I become more determined. So many times, I could have given up. I had every excuse to quit. I could have sat back and waited for new parts to be shipped in, or waited for a new compressor, or waited for someone else with the "right" experience to make a decision. In the end, Possibility Thinking was the key to success. ■

POSSIBILITY Coaching Session

If fear of making a mistake has paralyzed you or the company you work for, you are stunting your growth, and you will die

VOGANISM

An oops! is just one step closer to success.

on the vine. You know trouble is brewing when you hear or use these types of statements: *It's out of my control. It's not my responsibility. The other department didn't get me what I needed.* Nothing productive will come from this type of thought and action. Instead, disaster or paralysis will be waiting for the perfect moment to rear its ugly head.

One of the skills I teach—and encourage all of our clients to develop—is to discover problems and bring possible solutions to the table. I also encourage clients to think of these issues not as "problems," but as "opportunities." Through such thinking, you can encourage growth and innovation, rather than play the blame game. The blame game is long on accusations and short on solutions.

When we take on new companies as clients, we like to lead all the employees through a communication training process and lead the management team through leadership development. The training is designed to foster a change in the company culture. At every department meeting, we encourage managers to bring opportunities (problems) to open a discussion regarding potential solutions. In addition, the managers create an atmosphere where it is safe to bring up problems, admit mistakes, and together discover possible antidotes.

To start this process on your own, examine your method of examining and tackling problems. What do you say to yourself when you blow up your own compressor? How do you treat yourself when you make a mistake? If you are not making any mistakes, this might be thought of as a problem [opportunity], too. It means you are not taking any risks . . . and you and your company could be headed toward much bigger problems (not opportunities). Now, ask the same question about how you treat others when they make mistakes:

- How can you describe your personal, family, and company cultures today, insofar as problems and mistakes?

- Where do you want to step up your determination?

- As a leader, when you or your team wants to give up, what are you going to do to bring back the determination and persistence required to keep going?

- How can you replace the blame game with creative collaboration for creative solutions?

- How patient are you?

- Is there room for growth in the patience department?

 Yes, I know. There are many important questions. The gift is in discovering the answers.

Loss of KRYPTONITE

This story highlights the premise that you should never allow your dream to be shattered by someone else's decision or opinion. Learning to deal with unexpected setbacks, so that you are ready to rise to a challenge, is a continual growth process in life.

· ·

Superman finally shows up in September.

Then he leaves on Christmas Eve to go back to the U.S. to make more money, since our business is not profitable yet. Besides, he's having major mainland withdrawals. English-language radio broadcasts, television, and English-language newspapers are not yet available in Tonga. Over and over, he's reading the same sports page he brought with him. Back in America, he goes to El Pollo Loco every day to read the sports page and catch *Sports Center* on TV, with the regularity of tooth brushing. I learn he doesn't like to get dirty; getting a little engine oil on his hands seems the equivalent of the plague.

He promises to be back in a month. Now it's June, and he hasn't returned. Regular phone calls are far too expensive, so we start fighting through the fax machine. It's fun when the fax comes out on my end in Tonga, where I can only read half of it. It's like fighting in hieroglyphics! I'm living off of fish and rice for every meal, so I can send money home.

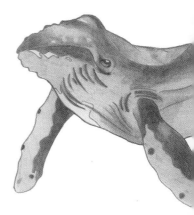

A phone call from a friend brings news that my husband has a girlfriend. He's been to Mexico with her three times in the past six months.

POSSIBILITY COACHING TIP:

When unforeseen circumstances hit you up side the head and rock your world, they can stop you in your tracks.

As you can imagine, this is the beginning of the end. It is the beginning of a more-determined me, relying only on myself to make my dream work, come hell or high water. He never returns to Tonga, and we get a divorce. It is my dream anyway, to have a dive shop in the tropics, so . . . I will live out my dream and do it on my own, though, truth be told, that's not my first choice. It wasn't that simple. I was devastated and heartbroken.

And that's what unforeseen circumstances do to me, personally and professionally. I have to dig down and find inner strength I sometimes don't realize I possess, if I am to keep the business going and deal with all my emotions at the same time. The shop is barely off the ground—or perhaps *afloat* is a better term to use. I push through the barriers and get a bank account opened as a single white female business owner—a first for the bank.

I am scared and many times think about folding it all up and going back home. Now, I recognize that such a difficult time in my life taught me the best lessons in determination and perseverance I had ever learned. I did not give up. Making decisions sometimes just required that I take the risk and do my best—and when it didn't work, just try it again. F.E.A.R. of making mistakes or doing something wrong was sometimes so very paralyzing that it took me forever just to start a project. The best I could do was the tropical version of: "Put one foot in front of the other," as I kept on swimming! The flip side was that every time I saw my dolphin friends, they gave me peace; they became a huge inspiration to me to keep going!

The next two years are very introspective for me. I had married for life, and I find the crushed dream a difficult pill to swallow. My heart is broken, and my ego is bruised. Yes, I know. I joked about Superman having the big ego; well, mine is not far behind. Humility can be very painful, but it has made me a better person, I hope. I look at my side of the street in the marriage, in my work, and in myself as a leader. Ouch! I am not as cool as I think I am. I am not perfect. I have a few warts, and I have learned many lessons. Remember the old adage: "You cannot see your reflection in rushing water." It takes that time, two years, for me to really look deep inside and see the real me and start to make some significant changes in my leadership style, to change the way I am showing up in the world. But first, I need to really look and discover my possibilities. What kind of leader do I want to be? What dreams do I have? What message do I want to send to the world?

Many adventures help me discover the importance of protecting the ocean and her children. With a team, I develop the first set of whale-watching rules with Fish and Game in Tonga. I pursue conservation efforts by taking on new roles: teaching kids about conservation, protecting the female lobsters, protecting the coral reefs by never dropping an anchor from our dive boats, educational programs with underwater slide shows, promoting tag and release for big game fishing in a huge and playful way, collaborating with other tour operators for the benefit of our businesses.

My possibility becomes clear!

It has taken tons of mistakes as a leader, learning from each blunder, and having the courage to make even more mistakes to discover my possibilities.

And I am still learning and striving every day to be a better person and leader. ■

POSSIBILITY COACHING TIP:

Making the same mistake a few times—before the lesson really sinks in—is really okay.

POSSIBILITY Coaching Session

VOGANISM

Fill the hole; become whole.

The Voganism above really hits home when you can paint the picture for yourself. Think of a time in your life when you experienced a painful problem or situation, one whose pain made you feel as though you had a hole inside of yourself—a big black bottomless hole filled with pain.

Filling the hole from the outside is a temporary fix or a Band-Aid. The hole is just going to get ripped open again when circumstances beyond your control arrive. What do your Band-Aids look like? Depending on your current life/business situation or the event that has really rocked your boat, your Band-Aid choices may be completely different. Such choices come in all shapes and sizes, obsessions taking over a healthy balance in your life. Obsessions with competitive sports, too much chocolate (if that is possible), diving head first into business and not looking up, too much alcohol, overeating, undereating, oversleeping, undersleeping, multiple sexual relationships, or too much of anything will only add to a life that is out of whack. No matter how you paint the picture, it will just be out of balance.

The alternative is to grab a shovel; just bury your hurt, and pretend all is well. Believe me, this is not better than a Band-Aid. The issue will resurface at some point—and probably not when you expect it.

The only permanent and healthy way to fill the hole within and become whole is to heal from the inside out. You need to admit to yourself why whatever occurred happened, deal with any issues that need to be dealt with, and open yourself up to discovering the possibilities this setback has created. And there are always possibilities.

"But," you say, "I hate this place I am in now. I can't stand feeling this way." What is the fastest way to heal and become whole again?" One of the fast tracks is to work with a professional therapist instead of just trying to figure it out on your own. We have a female and male therapist on the Victory Team to help leaders who have the courage to learn about themselves and heal from within, the courage to stop using Band-Aids. Still, visiting a therapist is not always possible. (One wasn't available to me on Tonga.) So, here are a few alternate ways for you to achieve clarity.

- **JOURNAL:**
  Many people find that writing in a journal is a very effective way to express their thoughts and feelings. In a week, they can re-read what they have written, and clarity will often emerge.

- **QUIET TIME:**
  We live in a time when every space is filled—with work, people, music, news, noise, and more noise. Be with yourself, calm

your mind. Limit as many outside distractions as possible, and concentrate on just breathing. Every time your mind wanders—and it will—just bring it back to your calm center, your breath. (You might be like I was, and you are saying as you read this, "Oh, give me a break. What is that supposed to fix? Who has time for sitting like Buddha and saying, Ohmmm?" You, my friend, are the perfect candidate!)

- **PERSONAL AND PROFESSIONAL GROWTH BOOKS:**
  Today, there are excellent books on many subjects, subjects such as personal and leadership growth and development. Remember that both parts—personal and business—must be considered together to create the "whole."

As a business coach, I have learned that leaders' uncovering and dealing with the "hole" has led to discovering their greatest strengths in the long run. The choice is always yours. How long do you want to continue relying on the Band-Aids? Do you have the desire to learn and grow? This is all it takes. Desire is a successful first step. Discovery is the second, and the ah-ha moments are a brilliant third.

Be a Human BEING, Not a Human DOING

Remember the famous words spoken by astronaut Jim Lovell from Apollo 13 to the ground crew? "Houston, we have a problem!" And Gene Kranz, the lead flight director for mission control, made another significant statement to the ground crew. "Failure is not an option." Our creativity does not always have the pleasure of emerging when we choose to feel creative. Sometimes, it is necessary to force ourselves to get creative or die. In order to shift our way of solving problems, we do not need a life-or-death situation, just a shift in our thinking. Note what happens to two people in this story who are facing the same problem. Pay attention to the differences in their problem-solving skills from the moment of discovery all the way through to solution.

. . . .

This story is about my little boat drinking too much petrol because it had a hole in the diaphragm of the 115hp Yamaha engine that I'd bought from Fata Fata Mafana, the local store where we could buy food, nails, oil, and outboard engines. Considering there was only one store in Vava'u, I'd figured it must carry the parts for this diaphragm thingy.

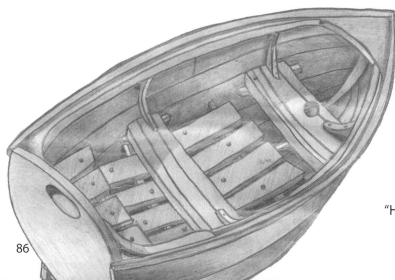

"No parts, Betty." The clerk shrugs apologetically.

"What do you mean, no parts? My boat cannot run." I try to regroup. "How soon can you get the part?"

"Maybe eight weeks?"

My heart sinks for just a moment as my mind races in a downward spiral to no diving, no money, no food, no fun, no life—failure! I go sulking back to the boat and tell Tomasi about my problem. He sends down Sione, a huge Tongan man with a gentle spirit, to look at my boat with me. He opens the hatch, takes off the lid, and stares at the engine. Following suit, I move in close and stare at the engine, too.

After two minutes that feel like two years, I ask, "What do you see?"

Silence.

So I wait . . . and ask again.

Nothing.

I wait at least a century. Has he fallen asleep with his big head in his oversized hand? Finally, my voice is an octave too high as I screech, "Sione, why are you just sitting there, staring at the engine? What are you doing?"

He walks away.

Oh, great! Now I've really pissed him off. I sit down on the side cushion of the boat, where it isn't so hot. I'm dripping in sweat, frustrated, angry at the situation, and angry at myself for losing it. I'm close to tears.

Sione comes waltzing back, holding a yellow rain coat. I roll my eyes; the sky is so blue that a cloud would not even feel welcome.

I think: *Does this idiot think it's going to rain? What is he doing, saying prayers over the boat?*

VOGANISM

Collective

consciousness

breeds

Possibility

Thinkers.

Hoping it will heal itself?

He brings out a pair of scissors and starts cutting up the rain coat. Now, I'm thinking, *Not only have I lost my mind, but so has he!*

I'm sure you've figured out by now that Sione doesn't talk much. He never explains what he's doing. I finally realize it's best to keep my mouth shut and watch. Amazing! In just a few minutes, he makes a new diaphragm from a rain coat.

He turns to me afterward and says, "Fixed, Betty."

I was still channeling *Ye of little faith*, saying something incredibly intelligent like, "How long will this thing last? A day or two?"

It turned out that my little boat ran better than ever, and Sione's invention lasted longer than a month, almost two, until the new part arrived. ■

POSSIBILITY Coaching Session

The beauty I found through living and running a business in a third-world country resulted in the expansion of Possibility Thinking that occurred for my staff and me. I've always been an optimist, a glass half-full, enthusiastic, driven type of person. Possibility Thinking has provided a step beyond all that. It's even beyond out-of-the-box thinking. Possibility Thinking connects to universal possibilities. I observed this with many of the Tongan people. I watched, learned from, and practiced their way of life, once I slowed down long enough to really get it. Possibility Thinking changed my life, and all the people who have worked in my company throughout the years have learned new ways of 'being' through Possibility Thinking.

How lazy have you become in your thinking and your being? Remember, we are human beings, not human doings. Notice how many times you think to yourself: *I—or we—can't do that because . . .* and I'm sure you are very good at coming up with numerous reasons why you cannot do something. The reasons are all valid, which helps to prove your point. How much finger-pointing is going on at the office that is associated with the I-Can't Camp? The finger-pointing might sound something like this: "I can't get the numbers to you because I am waiting for the other department to get me its information." Misery loves company, and the I-Can't Camp is always filled with people, though generally not very successful ones. What would happen if you switched your thinking to match the resourcefulness in Sione's thinking? What would happen if you sat in silence for a short period of time and thought only of the possible ways to make something happen? What will happen if you don't switch up your way of thinking? How long do you want to hang out in the I-Can't Camp"?

The opposite of Possibility Thinking is the I-Can't Camp. You might be interested to note how quickly I can get you to use the phrase *I can't* or *We (the office) can't!*

Ready?

Shut your business down for the day. Take the staff away somewhere, and create a Possibility Thinking Adventure Day. Don't say: "Oh no, can't do that . . . yada, yada, yada . . . "

Go pack your bags, your significant other's bags, and take your sweetheart away for a surprise weekend. Don't say: "We have too many obligations with kids, performances . . . yada, yada, yada . . ."

Take a personal vacation for yourself for three days. I can hear the I-can't excuse flying on that one.

Do something outrageous this weekend—skydiving, visiting a new restaurant, taking a hot air balloon ride, something you have never done. Don't say: "Not enough time to plan . . . blah, blah, blah . . . "

The point is for you to be aware of how quickly your mind moved to *can't, nope,* and *no,* instead of Possibility Thinking. How many times do you do this as a leader, and are you aware of it?

Possibility Thinking does not visit the I-Can't Camp. Instead, it goes beyond the normal types of solutions. This thinking creates possibilities built upon possibilities. The solutions are new and full of adventure, just waiting for a Possibility Thinker to discover them.

LESSON 12

JUNGLE Boat

It might seem to the developed world that people in third-world countries are judgmental and wary of innovation. The interesting thing is that I found just the opposite.

This third-world country, Kingdom of Tonga, is steeped in a tradition of living off of the sea. In fact, there is no word in the Tongan language that means "innovation."

In contrast, in developed countries such as the United States, where we think we are open-minded and on the cutting edge, I have seen that we can actually be barbaric in our judgments of others.

Sometimes, when you first hear it, a new and different idea seems laughable. A website where people will report about what they are doing, what they are thinking about, and what they had for lunch? No way! Well, millions of people aren't laughing at the idea of Facebook now!

When have you laughed at an idea someone came up with, called it stupid or impossible without a second of consideration? We have all done it on occasion in our professional or personal lives. As you read this story, reflect on what your judgments would be if you were one of the characters.

. . . .

For centuries, they have been long, thin, and smooth. They are best that way. Trying to convince him that much wider is better is much harder. A 60-minute conversation against 2,000 years of tradition is a difficult task, but I am getting more creative as the minutes tick by.

I start to draw my idea in the sand. Visuals always help me, so why not? Maybe it will help him to see that fatter really is better. The more the man draws in the air, using his broken English to say "sleek, smooth, fast." I use my broken Tongan to say BIG (in a deep voice, as though that makes it bigger). I'm saying "fat, huge, slow, stable, no move." The farther apart we get in words, the closer we get in spirit. I laugh at myself, and the man laughs right along with me.

Have you figured it out yet?

Most of the world does refer to our subject as female. It is a boat. We are talking about building a boat. You see, in Tonga, it is important to cut through the water efficiently to conserve petrol. Ancestors of modern-day Tongans built their boats small and fast to conserve human power. Today, a boat sports an outboard engine, possibly two, if you get really fancy. The boats are not very wide at all. Their slight, 2-meter-wide beam makes them low to the water line, cutting down on wind resistance, so they speed through the water.

In Tongan culture, the male role is fisherman. Fishermen travel far out to sea in their minimal shelter pine boats, each boat with one small outboard engine on the back, and they return with an incredible catch.

Imagine me, a white-skinned, petite, blonde American woman talking to the best boatbuilder in all of Vava'u about how to build a boat. Just think about it. I'm asking for him to design everything to be opposite of what he knows is the best. What is a man like that to do? It's a good thing that he is polite. In some countries and cultures, the Head Honcho (CEO, VP, Person in Charge) would not have even given me the time of day, let alone entertained any new ideas when I didn't have the correct background or proven skills. How many times have you not even listened because of your pre-judgment of other people? You say to yourself, *They know nothing about our industry; they can't help!*

The fat humpback picture in my sand drawing starts to look a bit more like a boat. I can't pronounce Tou poalokiiani's name correctly, so I just refer to him as The Captain. The Captain finds a shell and a piece of wood from a nearby tree. He starts to carve the piece of wood into the shape of my picture from the sand, creating a blueprint of my boat. As he carves, I explain that I want a "fat" boat. I try to illustrate how we're going to use the boat for scuba diving, whale watching, and sport fishing.

Out of the three activities I list, guess what he hears? Fishing—and fishing only. That starts us down the thin-versus-fat conversation again. I need stability, but Tongan boats are made to move. Dive boats and whale watching charters spend a great deal of time drifting with the current. The boats can't be tippy when people move from one side to another. When I start to explain to The Captain why I want a 4-meter beam, twice as wide as the beams he is accustomed to building, I realize he has no idea about scuba diving as a vacation sport. So, I try to explain.

The closest thing he can relate to is seeing some of the younger fishermen get a mask and fins to free-dive for sea cucumbers. (They sell the sea cucumbers to make money.) Scuba diving, though? He's never seen anyone use a tank before. And whale watching just makes him laugh. We Pa'alangi people amuse The Captain to no end. Why sit in the hot sun to look at big fat fish when you can sit on island

93

under a palm tree with a breeze—and take a nap while fish cook in the umu?

As the boat takes to frame, I hike back into the jungle to visit the boat and The Captain. We finally agree, after all of our negotiating over a size equivalent, to 12 meters (36 feet) long with a 4-meter (12–foot) beam. She will be built of New Zealand pine and copper nails. The hull will be royal blue and the rest white, sporting the Dolphin Pacific Diving logo on each side. Her name will be Dolphin Diver. I can picture myself at the helm, hearing the energized chatter from twenty divers as we head back to the resort after a day at sea.

The time comes for determining price and delivery. No, not to pay The Captain. Just for the cost of the materials. I order the pine and other required materials from New Zealand. Tonga is, of course, very limited insofar as availability of supplies. The most expeditious way to get the material is to find someone else who needs items from New Zealand. After doing so, I must power through the negotiation process and logistical organization as I try to keep the process from turning into a nightmare.

The company where I buy the pine doesn't have copper nails. That would be too easy. Copper stilettos . . . yeah, I know just where to find those. I don't have a clue where to start. My friends, Julia and John-Boy, have a friend from England who just happens to be visiting Vava'u two weeks before the wood will be delivered. They pull out their best negotiation skills, or perhaps I should say bartering skills. Their friend will bring as many nails as possible, and I will teach him and his wife to scuba dive in return. Seems a fair delivery fee to me, and of course I'll throw in a round of beers. But that's a whole different story . . . ∎

POSSIBILITY Coaching Session

In this coaching session, I would ask questions about who you are as a leader today. Let's take a quick trip back in time. When you were a kid, what did you want to be when you grew up? When you were a teenager, what did you want to do? In high school, did you think about an invention or idea, but found yourself afraid to act on it because everyone would think of it as stupid? Tell me about a time when your thoughts, dreams, and ideas were derailed by someone else's judgments. How did that change your course or direction in life? If you have children of your own, when have you been judgmental with them? Today, as a leader, how judgmental are you of yourself first and then others? Give me some examples of situations in which you have stopped yourself from going forward due to your own judgments. From as recently as last week, find examples of how you judged yourself or others, as well as examples of times you were open and receptive to new or different ideas.

I know these questions are not easy to answer, and being open and honest with yourself can be difficult. Only the brave and courageous can answer these types of questions. Because of this, the important stuff in life often is left unexplored. Take a deep breath. Then spend a little time answering these questions, and you will become more aware of how judgmental you are. Using a journal to capture your answers is one way to get started. Hire a coach. Use the questions for dinner conversation with others who are brave enough to open up and explore judgments. A good bottle of wine just might help out here.

VOGANISM

The number-one killer of creativity is judgment.

Spirit of SERVICE

These days, good customer service sometimes seems like a lost art. It takes too much effort for you to get support to understand your problem or your needs. The customer service solution is convoluted and cumbersome. And eventually, after a few tries, customer service reps tell you it's the other guys fault, and they can't do anything for you. What?!

So often, companies put no effort into this very important aspect of the business, but it could be the very thing that causes a business to win an account from the competition. When your customers feel as though you really understand their needs, wants and desires, that you are an ally and are going to make things easier for them, then you will get their business. When you stop selling and come to the relationship with a spirit of service, then you become the customer's powerful partner.

This story explains just how special customer service can be and what a huge difference it can make in the lives of your customers, even changing their lives and yours.

. . . .

I have a core belief that when people are on vacation, they should be treated as if they are the King and Queen of Holiday. At Dolphin Pacific Diving, we are known as the champagne dive company of the South Pacific, due to our high standards of customer service. In the South Pacific, people would use the term, *island time*, which equates to unreliable, late, fickle, and a few others descriptive adjectives I am sure you can come up with all on your own. That is not the case for Dolphin Pacific Diving (DPD). It is standard for workers in our business to be early or on time. It is okay if the tourist is late, but never the DPD staff.

There are only three companies in the islands that make their employees wear uniforms. One is the National Reserve Bank of Tonga, the second is the Moorings Yacht Charter Company, and

the third is Dolphin Pacific Diving. The customer service of each employee is extraordinary from the inside out, and the outside reflects the inside heart of the employee: clean, pure, and ready to be of service.

The care we take of the boats also reflects the spirit of service. They are cleaned before and after each charter. The staff memorizes the names of the guest divers and introduces the guests to each other to create a welcoming and fun atmosphere.

When you step onto one of the Dolphin Pacific's boats, whether you are a diver, a whale watcher, a fisherman, or just a passenger, you become the King or Queen of Holiday. We wait on you hand, foot, and fin, to be precise. Our guests never have to lift or carry a piece of equipment from the moment they embark to the moment they debark. The staff anticipates guests' needs. Staff are even happy to bend over and put on guests' fins.

After the dive, staff lifts all of guests' equipment for them and changes the tanks while guests nibble fresh fruit and coconut, and sip something wonderful to drink. We point out the wonders of the underwater world and take the pictures if the guests don't want to do it themselves. At the end of the day, the staff clean all the guests' dive gear and return it to their rooms or keep it in the dive shop, if the guest prefers. If a staff member sees one of our guests relaxing at the resort under a palm tree with a drink that is almost finished, the staff member will walk over and refresh it before the guest can ask.

In the scuba diving world, safety is part of customer service, too, and especially important to me. Our standards are extremely high. We never leave our boats unattended. We have a dedicated boat driver, as well as dive masters and instructors on board when necessary. We also do not anchor the boat, as it is important to all of us to act as environmentalists and protect the coral.

There is not a hyperbaric chamber in the kingdom. In fact, New Zealand has the closest chamber, and that is a long ways away! Therefore, we always have all the appropriate safety equipment. In fact, the hospital has to borrow our oxygen units from time to time when the hospital runs out of its own!

We believe that we should treat our customers as if they are guests in our own homes. Not everyone treats guests in their homes the same way, so at the staff meetings we talk about how each staff member can accomplish this goal, and then we talk about the expectations of the company and how to fill in the gaps when they occur.

POSSIBILITY COACHING TIP:

I only hire employees who have the spirit of service within them, and it must shine through every aspect of their jobs. This potential is something I look for during the interview process. The applicant has to smile (such an important skill!), be personable, open, and friendly, and be in tune with the needs of customers. One of the questions I ask during the interview is to describe their philanthropic experiences. I want to know what type of volunteer work they have done and how those experiences have affected their lives. If an applicant can't demonstrate a desire to serve others, he or she is not a good fit for my company. They also must understand that our team philosophy is that nothing is beneath any of us.

In the case of Dolphin Pacific Diving, interviewing is a huge responsibility for me, because I am asking some applicants to move to a new country to work for me. In addition, I have to vouch for them so they can get work visas and permits. Essentially, I am stating that they are going to be upstanding citizens while they are in Tonga.

Everyday we look for ways we can serve, ways that go above and beyond. On one occasion, two of our instructors gave dive lessons to a woman who could not walk without crutches. They spent extra time and energy helping her learn to dive, but would not accept extra pay. One of the instructors said it was more rewarding than any amount of money to help this woman experience true freedom in the water, where her disability didn't matter. After her first dive, she and the instructor sat on the boat and cried together. The freedom of floating through the water and feeling weightless was like flying to her. The instructors truly gave her a holiday gift of freedom and made her feel like the Queen of Holiday.

On another occasion, we had a father and son who were sailing around the world together. They built this incredible steel-hulled sailboat in Ireland and now they were on a lifetime adventure. They came to the dive shop, saying they wanted to learn to dive. They both had severe hunchbacks. The majority of our backpacks (the apparatus that holds the tank to the body) are rigid and would not fit them. Two staff members loaned them their own soft backpacks for the week, so they could take class. No one asked the staff members to do it; they saw the need, and they offered.

A husband and wife came to the resort. The husband signed up to dive every day, but the wife did not. When we asked if she would like to try diving, we watched the blood drain from her face. She told us a horrifying story, explaining how she had gone through a dive course that was so bad, she'd almost died. She told us she was now afraid to put her face underwater even in the bathtub. That meant snorkeling was certainly out of the question. Day after day, her husband told her about all beautiful fish and coral he saw. It was obvious she wanted to be in the water with him and experience the same joy. I told her I would be happy to work with her in the water to help her get over her fears. We would not even talk about snorkeling or diving; we would just work on getting her comfortable in the water. Guess what? For the next nine days, while her husband was out diving, she and I worked together, step by step, swimming through her fears. On the last two days of their holiday, she went into the water for an extraordinary scuba dive with her husband.

In all these cases, we listened to our customers' needs. Good listening skills form the beginning of great customer service. We did it all with a smile and a laugh and the spirit of service. True customer service can be life-changing when people understand the meaning attached to the spirit of service. ■

POSSIBILITY Coaching Session

Tell me, what does customer service look like in your business? If I asked one of your customers to describe your customer service, what would that customer say? If I asked your co-workers or employees to describe occasions when they are demonstrating poor, average, and exceptional customer service, do you think they could do it—and recognize what the difference represents?

One of the biggest mistakes that companies make today is failing to pay attention to the first impression they make. Who is answering your phone? Who is the first face your customers see when they visit or are visited by your business? That person is not just the person who answers the phone or the sales guy. He or she is the Director of First Impression. How well does that person represent the company?

Beyond the first impression, customer service is the responsibility of every employee. What can each department and each person do to stand out from your competition in customer service?

The employees at The Ritz-Carlton Hotels have a core belief about themselves as employees. They all go through extensive customer service training before they start the job. Here is what all employees believe about themselves, and it shows: "We are Ladies and Gentlemen Serving Ladies and Gentlemen." Now, that speaks for itself.

What do all the employees in your office believe about themselves? Find out, either from them or from your customers.

Another of my favorite quotes is from Winston Churchill:

"We make a living by what we get, but we make a life by what we give."

In working with leaders of all ages, I often hear the comments about finding your purpose and making a difference, and then I hear the proverbial: "I can't make a difference. I am just one person." When you feel like this, remember the Starfish Story.

THE STARFISH STORY

Once upon a time, there was a wise man who used to go to the ocean to do his journal writing. He had a habit of walking on the beach before he began his work.

One day he was walking along the shore. As he looked down the beach, he saw a human figure moving like a dancer. He smiled to himself to think of someone who would dance to the day. So he began to walk faster to catch up.

As he got closer, he saw that it was a young girl and she wasn't dancing, but instead she was reaching down to the shore, picking up something and very gently throwing it into the ocean.

As he got closer he called out, "Good morning! What are you doing?" The young girl paused, looked up and replied, "Throwing starfish in the ocean."

"I guess I should have asked, why are you throwing starfish in the ocean?"

"The sun is up, and the tide is going out. And if I don't throw them in they'll die."

"But, young lady, don't you realize that there are miles and miles of beach, and starfish all along it. You can't possibly make a difference!"

The young girl listened politely, then bent down, picked up another starfish, and threw it into the sea, past the breaking waves and said, "I made a difference for that one."

There is something very special in each and every one of us. We have all been gifted with the ability to make a difference. And if we can become aware of that gift, we gain the power to shape the future through the strength of our visions and talents. We must each find our starfish. And if we throw our stars wisely and well, the world will be blessed.

VOGANISM

Use your God-given talents to serve others (1 Peter 4:10)

Each person could use whatever gift he has received to serve others, faithfully administering God's grace in its various forms.

A Brilliant AWAKENING

Sometimes even the boss needs to be reminded of the company standards when it comes to customer service. And even more importantly, the boss needs to remember that even though he pays his employees, they deserve the same respect you expect them to extend to your customers.

It finally took a couple of very loyal, caring employees to make me aware that I wasn't doing my job. That was a tough thing to hear.

When the truth comes out, how do you hear it? Do you deny that what you heard could possibly be true, or do you say, "Why didn't someone tell me this sooner?" This lesson explores why we sometimes don't find out until it's too late.

. . . .

I look at Kenny, my dive master, with a head tilted like a curious dog, and say, "What do you mean all the employees are unhappy? How could that be, when we have the highest ratings in customer service in the industry? We are busy, and everyone looks happy."

"It is not about their jobs, Patty. It is about the leadership in the company," he explains with a very straight face.

The business has grown; we started with one employee, and now we have nine. Our second dive boat, *Dolphin Diver*, is up and running. My goal in designing her was to have twenty divers roll off each side without the boat rocking from side to side. Although I initially had a lot of trouble explaining what I wanted, in the end, it worked!

This day, we are scurrying like mad men, getting ready for *Dolphin Diver*'s first big group —

eighteen divers from Texas, with us for two weeks. Just as soon as they leave, we have a big group of underwater photographers from New Zealand coming in to dive with us for a week. They are all big night divers, so we will be working in shifts for twenty-four hours a day. In addition, the regular busy season activity includes picking up divers from all over the islands, where they are anchored in idyllic coves on sailboats from the three yacht charter companies: Moorings, Rainbow, and Sailing Safaris.

The same week we have the photographers in, we will also have a flotilla of eight Moorings boats, with ten divers in that group. Here's the best part: the flotilla is a sector of the Mexican Mafia. I am not kidding. We will be bending over backward to meet their requests, mainly from fear of the outcome if we do not!

This crazy schedule will go on for the entire busy season, May to October. The crew seems at its best and happiest when we are really busy. What could go wrong?

POSSIBILITY COACHING TIP:

To make sure we had a stellar team, I asked everyone to read "The Color Code" by Dr. Taylor Hartman. His brilliant book demonstrates a way to profile personalities, and, in my opinion, it is the only book that really helps you to understand "motive." Why we do what we do? I only had two copies of the book, so everyone had to share. We tried to have bi-weekly meetings throughout the year to keep fresh all that we learned.

In "The Color Code", Dr. Hartman divides people into four personality types: red, blue, white, and yellow. Each type has its own set of innate strengths and limitations, as well as a motivating factor. Reds are motivated by power, Blues by intimacy, Whites by peace, and Yellows by fun. When you understand your color and realize that is how you were born, it really helps you and others to understand why you do what you do!

At the end of the second year, this great crew had two of the leaders, Kenny and Rose, sit me down to have a heart to heart. They told me they and the rest of the team did not like working for me anymore. I nearly fell off my chair. I really thought this was one of their practical jokes, but it was not. I was devastated. I thought I was a good leader, and I had pride in my leadership skills. Rose, a Blue — she could not lie even if she wanted to — and Kenny, a Yellow, said he was not having fun anymore and so he was over it.

They sat me down and used *The Color Code* to explain why I had unhappy employees. First, they assured me that no customer would ever know they were unhappy as a team. They really liked the work, the diving, and the customers; it was my leadership behaviors they no longer liked.

I was born a Yellow, and from early on, my motive has been fun! But when Kenny and Rose described how the team experienced me, it was not pretty, and my first reactions were defensive. As we continued to talk, I settled down and was able to listen. They said I was acting like a Red (power), with all the Red limitations and none of the Red strengths. I was negative, bossy, and demanding, and I had lost all of the Yellow, the enthusiastic, positive, fun side they had enjoyed.

At some point, deep inside my brain, I had decided that running a business needed to be "work" and that I needed to be miserable to be considered a serious business owner. To run a tight ship, I needed a whip instead of a feather boa. It took another season and the loss of a few good employees before I could change my actions and behavior. Kenny and Rose's Direct, Open, and Authentic (D.O.A.) communication was a real eye opener for me, but I still resisted the truth. Even though I intellectually "got it," it was not easy to turn around my behavior overnight and fix the damage I had already caused. I was very thankful that I had employees who felt strongly enough to have that conversation with me. The entire business could have died because of me if I hadn't had employees who were willing to take the risk. Thank you, Kenny and Rose.

Because all the staff had taken *The Color Code* profile, it was safer and easier for the two leaders to come tell me what was going on. It was easier for me to hear it because they were reminding me that my behaviors were not ringing true to my authentic self. That was easier to swallow than hearing that all the employees have no respect for me, think my management style stinks, and can't wait to get off the bloody boat and away from me! Ouch! That would have really hurt. ■

. . . .

POSSIBILITY Coaching Session

As a leader, you should be asking yourself, "Wow, I wonder how I am as a leader? I know my staff members are happy. At least, they tell me they are. But what do they really think of me as a leader?"

It's easy to dismiss that thought, isn't it? Of course, they tell YOU they are happy. What you really want to know is what they tell their family, friends, and co-workers about you.

Most people in business are scared to death to speak the truth. People are afraid of speaking the truth because they wonder what will happen if they communicate it in a hurtful way. They are fearful that if the receiver hears it in a hurtful way, then retaliation could be the consequence. Many employees take the stance of deciding it is better to just keep faking it and living the company lie than to risk the possible consequences of telling the truth.

That is why it is so helpful to use the wonderful personality and behaviorial assessment tools available to us, tools like *The Color Code, Everything DiSC Workplace,* and many others.

In our leadership company, we are trained to use many different types of tools that reflect behavior and personality styles, encouraging 360-degree feedback from all levels in the company.

It is much safer and actually much more accurate to talk about our communication differences in terms of personality or behavioral styles rather than being right or wrong or if I "like" you or don't "like" you. Any qualified business coach or leadership development company can help you identify the best tool for you to use in your company and for your desired outcome.

It is always advisable to use a professional facilitator to administer and interpret the results, so that confidentiality can be present. This will encourage the best opportunity for honesty and growth. In addition, a facilitator knows how to handle and manage all the personalities on the team.

Doing the same exercises as the rest of your team also makes you a team player, especially when you let the facilitator, not you, interpret the results — even your results. In others words, your kimono will be open, too. I have always said that my greatest growth comes from my greatest discomforts. When your motive is clean and true, take a step forward, and find the truth.

— VOGANISM —

We are never too old, too

set in our ways, or too successful,

to learn something new.

LESSON 15

All Work and No PLAY

How much farther do you expect your car to go when the gas tank indicator reads empty? Like all of us, you've probably run out of gas at least once or twice because you have been in a hurry to go somewhere, or you've had other interests on your mind, and you just haven't noticed the gas gauge. In the end, it is a total waste of time and energy to let a car run out of gas. And it isn't very good for the car, either.

Just like cars, we have indicators within our bodies that tell us when we are close to empty of energy, enthusiasm, whatever it takes to get through the day. And all too often, we ignore the signs and let ourselves run completely out of gas. What kind of leaders and partners are we when that happens?

In order for you to be a successful leader, you must learn to read, monitor, and understand your own "empty" indicators. They are uniquely yours. This story explains a few creative ways to refuel a person, rather than a car.

. . . .

It's hard to believe that two years have passed since Superman and I divorced. The expats call me the Unsociable One as a nickname, or at least that is the kind version, I am told. After Superman left, I spent my evenings at home alone, instead of at the local watering hole where most everyone landed. I was teaching myself underwater photography by day and developing slide film by night. If I planned to charge people to take pictures underwater, the pictures had better be really good.

I also spend my evenings creating marketing and sales packages that will bring groups of divers to Tonga. I work seven days a week; every day in Tonga is a weekend to the diver and tourist.

So what all this really means is that I stay home and work seven nights a week. I've never walked into a bar by myself, and I don't plan to start now. Chicken! It's not that I am above a local watering hole; I just do not want to do it alone. It's easier to stay busy with work than to try to create a social life.

One of the tourist divers tells me it's time for me to start dating, and I roar in laughter. Right, like who? Do you realize how small this island is? I know everyone. Eligible bachelors? Not.

This tourist is a beautiful British girl with a big heart. She tells me she is going to introduce me to an Australian man who is living in Nuku'alofa, the main island, someone she just met a few weeks ago. Since I have to go to Nuku'alofa anyway the next day, I agree to meet him.

In Nuku'alofa the following day, he walks up with his 6'3" frame, three axe handles across for shoulders, stunning blue eyes, and sandy blonde curly hair. He actually says with his charming accent, "G'day mate; my name is Grant." My green eyes sparkle with excitement, and I grin from ear to ear. I'll spare you the rest of the juicy details.

Grant ends up leaving his manufacturing business in Nuku'alofa and coming to live and work with me. He is a true Australian, loves the outdoors, and thinks beer is a replacement for water! He quickly makes friends and gets me out of the house and into the local watering hole. Grant helps me rediscover the beauty of balance between work and play.

. . . .

I'll never forget finally waterskiing to work for the first time. Our daily routine is to get to the dive shop via boat not truck. Being on time or early is not an easy chore for Grant and me. Even so, I decide it's really stupid not to waterski to work. I know if I don't do it once in a while, I'll regret it. Grant's at the helm of *Surface Interval*, the smaller predecessor to *Dolphin Diver*. I'm in the water, in classic water-ski pose: one ski on, left foot forward on the ski, nose of the ski pointed up, knees bent, hands stretched over my knees, gripping the towline. Grant accelerates quickly, and as I'm being pulled up onto the ski, I envision Interstate 5 back in the States, snarled with traffic, crashes, and smog. My sideways grin says it all.

The sky is intensely blue with white fluffy clouds; the water in the harbor is as smooth as glass, reflecting the sky. There's a bright pink hibiscus flower floating gently on top of the water as I ski by—a beautiful gift I don't ever want to forget. The closer we get to the Tongan Beach Resort, the more I think about my landing; I set it up in my mind. I want to look cool by coming in full speed on one ski and hanging a big rooster tail of water spray.

Mission accomplished! What a way to the start the day! We get the scuba gear ready in record time. Divers on the dock load up, and away we go for another wonderful day in paradise.

Grant and I continue to take turns waterskiing to work. Being on time becomes more fun. Sometimes, I really am just a kid.

. . . .

I don't know what it is about sailors, surfers, and people who live near the ocean; we appreciate the little things. Nature gives us gifts, and we don't take them for granted. A slight breeze when stuck in the doldrums, a ride in the barrel, or spotting a whale spout makes our day. With a carnival-like spirit, we take every opportunity to celebrate. That's the only explanation I can come up with for some of the bizarre parties I throw in Tonga.

My first official party honors the first birthday of my new dog, Bear. I invite about eight expats, respectfully requesting wrapped gifts for Bear-Dog. I prep for days, making party hats from leftover scraps of colored paper. Once we don them at the party, laughter comes hearty and hard when someone brings up the dunce-cap resemblance. Oh my, we look so stupid. Bear is in his glory with gifts ranging from an old grotty tennis shoe to a homemade wooden bone bearing his name.

The next month, we make another occasion out of a badminton tournament. Billy Bailey, the host, requests that everyone come costumed completely in white. We very properly drink gin and tonic while daintily munching on cucumber sandwiches. Everyone speaks with a fake British accent, except for the real Brits.

Eventually, even the colors pink and purple become a reason for a party. Pair a dress code with friends and cocktails, and all is right in my world. Sounds pretty stupid, but it's my release. Laughter is good for my soul. These little memories of simple, happy times in my life are most fulfilling. Life can be like a K.I.S.S. (Keep It Simple and Silly), if you let it. ■

POSSIBILITY Coaching Session

We are now sitting in my coaching office in San Clemente, California, overlooking the ocean. You tell me that you live in a fast-paced, highly stressed life filled to the brim with work, spouse, and kids—and even just the thought of finding space to create work-life balance is overwhelming! Catch 22.

Let's first take in a deep breath of ocean air and exhale all the stress that is clogging up your brain. Tell me about what you like to do just for fun. If you had no obligations, no to-do list screaming, "Finish me!" If you had no kids, chores, social commitments, etc. to pay attention to, what would you want to do? Please know that it's okay to say, "I do not have a clue." I often hear that statement. Just open your mind, and allow any answer to come out.

This is where we would start to learn how to create a refueling program for you. Everybody has a figurative gas tank, and we all need to fill it.

- How long has your gas tank been running on empty?

- What have you done in the past to fill 'er up?

- If so, how often? And is this method working for you?

There are four important keys to creating a successful refueling process that will create sustainable energy for you in the face of increasing demands. The keys to success consist of looking at your life as it relates to four aspects: physical, mental, emotional, and

> ## VOGANISM
>
> *All work and no play*
>
> *makes for one long, boring day!*

spiritual. You will learn which areas are low in fuel, and then we can create refueling stations for you in those areas. Keep in mind, though, that most people need refueling in all four areas, some just more often than others. We have created these types of "energy" programs for entire companies, as well as executives, and these programs have given everyone more energy and a more creative, more resourceful, more productive attitude.

The One That DIDN'T Get Away

This story is about having your back up against a wall and being required to do something you do not want to do at all. Sometimes as leaders, we are forced to make really difficult decisions in life, decisions that go against all our beliefs. It is important to remember that rules, even those you create yourself, under certain circumstances, might need to be bent.

. . . .

Six A.M.. The ice chests are full of fresh fruit, sandwiches, and drinks, the rods and reels are sparkling clean, and the engines are all running. The prize money is big; the competition is fierce. And anticipation is building! This is serious business to all the fishing teams—except one. The Double-Barreled Slingshots (made up of Samantha, Maureen, and me) are the first all-female team in the history of the Vava'u International Bill Fishing Tournament. Grant is our captain, steering the boat, though he's not allowed to help us fish. We're not sure what adventures the next three days will bring, but whatever happens, our main goal will be to have fun.

As the sun rises, the Double-Barreled Slingshots don our gear—size 44 triple-F red bras, stuffed with socks and worn on the outside of our tee-shirts. All three women climb to the front of the boat, waving and shouting, "Good luck, boys!" We shimmy our brilliant red double-barreled slingshots as we cruise by each boat. It is obvious from their reactions that the men don't know what to think of this addition to the annual contest.

Forty-five minutes later, all the fishing teams are at their "magic" spots, outriggers in place, lines looking good, lures running smoothly and popping up in perfect harmony as they troll the deep blue Pacific for the big one. Each team checks in on the VHF radio periodically. It is mandatory to report a strike, and of course, you gloat across the airwaves when you land one.

Just for fun, I start a quiz on the VHF radio. "In three seconds, there will be a sound. Let's see who can identify it correctly." Pop goes the cork to our bottle of champagne, and on cue, we women shout: "Cheers!"

"What is that sound, gentlemen?" I say into the radio, with a smirk in my voice. Some of the men respond with laughter and a patronizing, "Have fun, you silly girls!" The serious competitors offer words of encouragement, such as "Don't drink too much, or you will get sick!"

At the end of each day during the tournament, everyone gathers around the weigh-in station to see who has caught the biggest bill fish, blue, black, or striped marlin. The fish are hung by their tails from the scale and left for all to admire, while the fishermen's stories become more dramatic and colorful with each display.

In addition to having creating the very first set of whale watching regulations in Tonga, I am the Kingdom's most passionate advocate of tag and release. In this competition, the fishermen who tag a marlin and release it can actually get more points. Sadly, there is nothing to show at the end of the day as the tag and releasers' stories are told.

So this year, I decide to create a way for the tag and releasers to enjoy as much glory as the others. I ask Sherri, an incredible artist and one of the world cruisers moored in our harbor, if she and her husband Larry would create a huge plywood marlin cutout, painted in glorious blue, a happy cartoon character of a marlin. They agree, and in just a few days, Merlin the Marlin is born!

The Merlin cutout stands taller than 7 feet. Merlin has a big happy smile and bright eyes, and his pectoral fin is so large that it extends beyond the shoulder of the fishermen who stand next to it to get their pictures taken. There's a chalkboard at the bottom of the Merlin cutout. There, we write all the important information for the contest: weight, length, species, line class, etc.

After the first day, it is clear that Merlin is a huge success. The fishermen love Merlin! By the second day of the competition, all the competitors (tag and release or not) are making sure they get their pictures taken with Merlin the Marlin.

We run through our red-bra "Good Morning, Boys!" routine every morning. By the third day, the other teams are hooting and hollering and banging on their chests, Tarzan-style, as we cruise by. What a sight!

Although we'd not had a chance to demonstrate our fishing skills on day one, by the end of day two, we've tagged and released two marlin. The long-time competitors can hardly believe the fact that these silly, bra-bearing girls are in the running.

The third day arrives, and the competition is wide open; anyone can win. The weather has turned against all of us, the seas getting rougher as the winds continue to build. The Double Barreled Slingshots are fishing out of *Surface Interval*, my first dive boat. An 18-foot-long runabout with a 115hp Yamaha and no back-up engine, she is the smallest boat in the competition. We are grateful to Grant, our trusty captain, for his skill at the helm.

We tag and release a beautiful blue in the morning, before the weather gets too rough. The waves are getting so big now that our little boat is surfing them, and we are grateful that

Grant can hit them just right. We are running four lines off the back of the boat, and they are pulling so hard on the drag that each line sounds like we are getting a strike as we surf down the waves. We hear Zzzzzzzz with the downward motion of each wave.

The little boat is tossing back and forth, and it is getting harder to manage the boat, the lines, and ourselves. We've all lost our balance at some point and have bruises from banging into the sides of the boat. We realize we are in the danger zone, that someone could really get hurt or fall off of the boat—and we are in the middle of Tonga Trench, the area where the big sharks live.

At the moment we decide to turn around and head back in, zing! We get a strike, and we are hooked up! Grant is steering the boat and shouting orders. Maureen is helping Samantha (whose turn it is to reel in the fish) get organized and stable to fight the fish in the stand-up position; we do not have a fighting chair. I quickly pull in the other lines and secure the rods and make sure the lures are safe, so they won't impale any of us.

Sam is doing great, even though she has been fighting the fish for forty-five minutes, and sweat is dripping down her face. I radio in an update on our hook-up with excitement, and I get encouragement from our newly developed fan club. I have the tag-and-release equipment all set up, and I am so excited that there is no way I am going to miss tagging this fish.

WOW! NO Way! Look at that! The marlin is tail walking all over the place. Maureen and I scream at Sam, "Reel, reel." Sam keeps a cool head and holds steady, fighting her own fish and ignoring us crazies. In no time, this stunning marlin is up next to the side of the boat. I grab the tag-and-release pole, and with all my force, tag the marlin right behind the dorsal fin in the perfect spot! It is such a shock to the marlin that he shakes his head, spits out the hooks, and nose- dives for the depths.

We are all jumping up and down and high-fiving each other when we hear Grant scream, "Oh, no!" We turn, and to our utter amazement, watch this massive marlin jump out of the deep water, high into the air, and land in the boat!

Now, there is one huge, really mad marlin jumping and thrashing all over the boat! "Oh, my God!" Maureen screams hysterically and jumps on top of the VHF radio box like a stereotypical woman afraid of a mouse. The marlin's bill is like a knife out of control as it slashes against Samantha's leg, creating an open gash on her calf. She winces in pain as she climbs onto the side of the boat, about ready to fall into the ocean. The boat is pushed over by a huge wave and is ready to capsize. Grant rushes to the wheel and screams at me to get the Louisville Slugger® baseball bat we always keep on board for moments like this— though we've never had to use it before. The marlin thrashes back and forth, its bill slicing everything in sight. Somehow, it jets forward, and the bill pierces the side of my knee. It moves on and rips open the newly upholstered seat cushions. Its scales—with needles on the ends—are flying everywhere and getting into our bare feet. We work through the pain.

As Grant maneuvers the boat downwind, I grab the bat and start hitting the fish over the head. Grant leaves the wheel and jumps on the fish; rides it as if it were a bull. I beat the fish over and over, trying my best not to hit Grant. Blood splatters everywhere, even hitting me in the face. I hate beating this fish, but I have no choice. I have to kill it, or it is going to kill one—or all—of us. I begin to cry hysterically between blows. "Just die, you bastard!," I shout.

Finally, I hear Grant yelling, "It's done; it's done. It's dead. Stop, Patty, stop!" I fall down in a puddle of blood, still gripping the bat. I sob and tell the marlin I am so sorry I had to kill it.

We drift for a while in silence, everyone exhausted and covered in blood. Then Grant fires up the engine, and we head for the first sheltered place we can find, so we can get the boat organized and collect ourselves. I radio the event into headquarters, and the rest of the fishermen —even the grumpy ones—offer to come to our aid. They can tell by my voice that this time, I am not joking.

At the awards ceremony that night, we three girls hobble up to the stage and receive a standing ovation for our passion and efforts. In return, we share this poem we wrote of our adventure.

AND THEN IT HAPPENED

There was a young couple in '93 who went out fishing on the deep blue sea,
It was so hot they took off their clothes and, lo and behold, a big marlin arose . . .
AND THEN IT HAPPENED.

The same young couple in '94 were ready to pack up at quarter to four
When along came a Blue of enormous size and, blow me down, they won a prize . . .
AND THEN IT HAPPENED.

In '95 these same two had a dream, "Why don't we make up a Ladies Team?"
So Turner and Cooch came from afar and brought with them a few red bras . . .
AND THEN IT HAPPENED.

We had to prove ourselves to the boys who had the big boats and flashy toys.
It took all week to practice our tricks - we all came back with plenty of licks . . .
AND THEN IT HAPPENED.

The last day dawned rough and red, we were all confident we could get ahead
When Sam hooked a marlin and reeled it in we all thought MAYBE this one could win . . .
AND THEN IT HAPPENED.

As cool and calm as we could be we hauled that sucker right out of the sea,
We tagged and released and were about to gloat
When the bloody thing jumped into the boat . . .
AND THEN IT HAPPENED.

All hell broke loose and we all took flight as this angry black marlin continued to fight.
Blood, guts and scales went all over the place and a look of fear was on everyone's face.
AND THEN IT HAPPENED.

Grant yelled at Patty to grab the slugger.
She finally found it and whacked the bugger.
She finished him off once and for all and we all realized we'd had a close call . . .
WHEN IT HAPPENED.

PS: Just one more small thing we'd like to add
For all you keen chaps who fish at the FAD,
You all know what a red rag does to a bull
If you wear a red bra—you'll catch your marlin on the full!!

The moral of our little story must be
That when you go fishing on the Tongan sea
If you want to tag your fish and weigh it too,
You have to let it jump in the boat with you.
It's called having your cake and eating it too!!!

Poem from the Double Barreled Slingshot Team,
The first All Ladies Team in the T.G.I.F.A., October 1995.

Dedicated to Grant Harris, our Skipper, the bravest man in Tonga! ■

POSSIBILITY Coaching Session

No matter how hard you try, you sometimes don't get what you want; you get what you need. Sometimes, things just go wrong, and you must abandon rational thought and do what you have to do. You know you are in a tough place, but can't stop and contemplate "Why, oh why did this happen?" You just have to act.

> ## VOGANISM
>
> It's not how many times I fall or how many mistakes I make that counts; it's how many times I get back up that matters.

I created Merlin the Marlin, the seven-foot-tall cartoon character, to promote tag and release in the tournament. That was a good thing, and I felt great about doing it. Then, why on earth did I have to be the one who ended up killing a fish with a baseball bat? In this case, I think I had to do what I needed to do to protect my friends, even if it meant compromising values that I hold so dear and believe in so much.

One of my clients found himself facing a very difficult decision to make in his family-run company. He discovered that his own son had been stealing from the company. He was heartbroken first, then angry, and he did not know what to do. He had given his son the best of everything and brought him up in a loving home, and he hoped his son would one day take over the family business. Now, he was faced with this heart-breaking situation.

In his mind, he had only two choices, to tell his son he knew what was going on and give him a warning, or to turn him over to the police. He chose to turn him over to the police. It was the hardest decision he had ever had to make, but he also knew that it was the best decision for the company and the other family members who worked there, as well all the employees and ultimately, his son.

If your back is against the wall and you do not know what to do, first get help if you can. Here are a few ideas to consider next:

- If the matter is time critical, forget about figuring out how you got here. Focus on the problem and how you are going to handle it.

- Think of all the possible actions you could take. Then imagine the outcomes and determine which feels best to you. "If I take option A, this is what it will look like at the end, and if I take Option B, the outcome will be different because of these specific variables." If you have never been one to trust your gut, this might be a time to try—because your gut is often right.

- How many lives will this decision affect, and exactly what impact will it have on those lives? What will cause the least amount of harm to the greatest number of people?

- How will this affect your company and/or family in the short term and the long run?

- If no one else were involved, what decision would you make?

Unfortunately, we sometimes in life must do things that go against our grain. We find ourselves making very difficult choices. No one can ever fault you for giving your all and doing your best. If you choose to do nothing, that is, in fact, a choice. Remember, you are smart; you are powerful, and you make a difference in this world with your individual style of leadership. Always give it your all and do your best. That is all God will ever ask of you.

When ALL Is Said and Done . . .

So many times in business, we act and react as if the problems and issues we are facing are life threatening. Are they really? Usually not.

Dr. Norman Vincent Peale said, "Don't you trust me anymore, Lord? Please give me some problems." He was a believer in taking problems and shaping them up as a means to a good end. He also once said, "You've got problems? Be glad you've got them. Hang onto them as long as you can, for when they're gone, unhappily you're gone!"

Unfortunately, it sometimes actually takes a life-threatening situation in our lives to get us to wake up and smell the importance of problems and challenges. This story brings out an attitude of gratitude.

. . . .

Lying next to Grant in bed, I marvel at the dry sheets: no fever sweat. Grant's breathing comes in an even rhythm. I match his cadence. In, out. In, out. Yep, it's regular. His screams, the unbearable itching, his wishes for death to take him . . . lost to the silence. He's finally over the dengue fever. I hear only the tick of the antiquated wall clock. Am I the one hallucinating? I hover my fingers over his mouth to feel his breath. So many times in the past two weeks, I've wished for "regular." So many times, I've yearned for an easy night of sleep.

Now, I can't sleep. And that bugs me. I want to drape myself over his sturdy torso and hold him—to place my head on his chest so I can hear his heartbeat. I'm torn because I don't want to wake him. So, I turn on my side toward him and hug my pillow instead. Tonight, I know Grant will wake up in the morning. I'm sure of it. The certainty should give me solace, not insomnia. I must be too tired to sleep.

It's the clock. I'm hearing it tick. I don't want to waste any more ticks of the clock. I want to see the sunrise. Not just watch it. I want to experience it. Feel the day turn from cool to warm. See the spray when the waves crash. Hear the birds welcome the day. The bugs? I'm still gonna' smash 'em.

. . . .

A few weeks later, Grant waltzes into the dive shop, looking smug. Dengue fever, shmengue fever, he's back to his happy healthy self.

He tells me, "We're heading to dinner with Eduardo and Maria." He knows I think they are freaks. He's taking advantage of my new "live for the moment" plan.

"Oh, we are, are we?" I smile back at him, mentally going through my list of excuses. The next dive group, the next dollar, the next everything used to seem so important.

He's waiting for it, waiting for my no. His smile dares me to say it.

I stick out my tongue. "Well, we'd better bring them some cold beer, then." Right now, I just want to be with Grant. If he's going to the freaky Spaniard Island, then I'm going, too.

We take our little boat, *Surface Interval*, way out to one of the deserted islands, Tapana.

Tomasi had taken me out there for dinner once when I'd first moved to Tonga. My impressions from that night had prevented me from returning. The couple lived off the island, Blue Lagoon style, in a hut made of driftwood and palm fronds. Taking a freshwater shower would be a waste of water to them. Their carefree ways proved too lazy for me. I had goals. I had a business to run. I didn't want their island fever to rub off on me. After dinner, Eduardo sang and played his guitar. He was the worst singer I'd ever heard. Enduring the strange couple through the meal had been worth it, though, because the full moon rose while we ate. Tomasi had rewarded my patience with a night sail. I can still see the beautiful silver sea and hear the lapping of the ocean on the side of the boat. I can still feel the wind catching in the sails. Of course, Tomasi and I were friends but at that very moment I had wished we were lovers. It was a most beautiful, romantic evening. The wind had called for making love under the moonlight.

The outboard engine of *Surface Interval* roars me back to the moment. I pull my windbreaker tight around me, as Grant steers us through the slight chop and shallow coral heads. I relish feeling cold; it's such a rare occurrence on a tropical island. The combination of sunset, spray flying over the bow, and wind in our faces makes for actual goosebump conditions. I look up to see if there's a full moon anywhere in sight.

"Maria, how do you make this taste so good with so little to cook with?" I marvel at her during dinner. Her paella tastes better than I remember, and it certainly draws a crowd, judging by the group of ten or so people sitting on the driftwood logs around the campfire with us. She shrugs and offers everyone rainwater to drink; it's their only source of fresh water. I stick with the warm beer, as do the other sailors. By the time Eduardo plays his guitar, I find it easy to ignore his off-key singing.

Pretty soon, someone else joins in with a homemade instrument that looks like a washboard. Plastic buckets turned upside down transform into drums. The more I drink, the better they sound. Before long, I'm acting like a rock star playing the drums. It occurs to me that I might be the real freak. This couple gets the meaning of living in the present moment, truly experiencing life, and choosing to enjoy it—however it comes. Sometimes, it is good to just let go and believe. It makes me wonder how many other times my judgmental attitude has stopped me from having a magical experience in life.

. . . .

On a typical sport-fishing excursion, Grant gets the gear ready and captains *Dolphin Diver*. I'm there to help the tourists, check their lures, serve as tour guide, try to sell them on scuba diving, and generally serve as first mate.

The Tonga Trench is one of the world's deepest underwater canyons, second only to the Mariana Trench. Any time there are great depths adjacent to tropical shallows, there's an abundance of sea life and the opportunity to see rare sights.

Another benefit of this peculiarity is incredible sport fishing. A present-day international game fishing lodge, Ika Lahi, touts its translation "Big Fish—Many Fish." These are waters where game fishermen hunt for marlin and sailfish throughout the year. This isn't the kind of fishing where one drops down a line and waits for a bite. *Trolling* is the term used to describe running fishing lines off the stern of the boat, letting them trail behind as the boat is underway. It's the best way to catch big game fish, as well as good "eating fish," like yellowfin tuna, mahi mahi, and wahoo.

Spotting marine animals is an art. Looking out onto the horizon, dolphins have a distinctive splash. When there's a pod, the ocean from a distance looks like a bubbling Jacuzzi®. As you move closer, dorsal fins become visible. Closer still, and tourists can pick out a few jumpers— playful dolphins twirling in the air and leaping from swell to swell. One might expect boats to scare them away. On the contrary, boats are dolphin magnets. Dolphins redirect themselves for a chance to race the boat and play in the bow waves. This view is close-up enough for many travelers. Feeling a little splash from the blowhole, hearing the clicks and whistles, and feeling the animal almost within reach provide thrill enough.

But not for me. Grant and I have an agreement when we're out fishing for fun, not charter. When we come across dolphins or whales, we pull in the lines, so I can jump in and have a play with them. I'm crazed with affection for these gentle animals. I'm this way every time. My wonder and enjoyment never diminish; it's always as good as the first time. It's almost like seeing a long-lost relative I dearly love, or an old friend. We pick up wherever we left off, and it feels as though no time has passed. I don't know why, but my connection to dolphins and whales feels exceptionally special. It's not something I created. It just is.

Spotting whales is different than spotting dolphins. The ocean doesn't look interrupted. It looks still. Even the most careful lookout will just see the spray, not a real spout of water like a fountain. It looks like a puff of foggy air, like when you can see your breath on a frosty morning. It hangs above the water for a moment before dissipating. With humpbacks in the tropics, one might have the added delight of seeing fins, flukes, and very rarely, spyhopping or breaches. The whale's fluke, also called the whale's tail, provides the means of identifying an individual whale. The underside of the whale fluke is similar to the human fingerprint, in that each one is unique in pattern. The whales hanging out in Tonga for the season are those traveling up from the Antarctic. Their flukes have a great deal more white on them than the humpbacks' flukes I've seen in Hawaii as they've traveled from Alaska.

On this particular day, we see dolphins jumping and a whale breaching. Astonishing. This never happens. Then another breach. Wow! One right after another, jumping vertically, high in the air, and splashing down sideways with a huge crash. I squeal with excitement and say, "Let's pull in the lines and go play. I can't believe it, dolphins and whales at the same time. Woo-hoo, what a treat!"

When we get close, Grant slows the boat. I'm running from side to side near the stern, looking down through the crystal-clear waters to see the whales turning upside down and swimming under the boat. Their white bellies are so beautiful; in the blue water they become a color not yet named by man or woman. *Dolphin Diver* looks like a whale herself from underwater. I remember the first time I went diving off of her. We were about thirty feet below, and I looked back up toward the surface. The boat takes the shape of a whale from an underwater view, due to the wide beam. I believe this is why whales always come to us when we're nearby and just drifting.

The first two whales swimming under the boat are upside down, with their white bellies toward the surface. Off the bow of *Dolphin Diver* are three more whales resting on the surface with dolphins all around them, swimming, jumping up, and spinning. There are two types of dolphins today—spinners and bottlenose—which is amazing in itself.

I'm so excited, because my dolphin friends are here, and so are the whales. How could I be so lucky? Of course, we'd only planned to fish today, not dive, so I don't have any of my gear. However, I do have my underwater camera. I search the boat for a mask, snorkel, and fins. Sometimes, the dive masters stuff them in a hideaway spot for backup. I find one mask. No snorkel. No fins. The mask is a child's mask. So what? I will make it work. I only have my string bikini on, a child's mask squishing my face, and my camera with no lanyard.

I gently lower myself into the water. Taking a breath, I place my face under the surface and look all around me. There are dolphins below me, beside me, ahead of me, and everywhere around me. I think I must be in heaven. I don't want to lift my head to take another breath, because I might miss something. I look about 100 yards ahead of me and see two whales swimming underwater. I lift my head and tell Grant I'm going to swim over to them in front of the boat. I don't have fins, but I do have powerful swimming legs. I hold the camera close to my body, take a breath, and put my face back in the water. I kick my legs, of course, being very careful to kick underwater with no splash. I always swim like that on the surface of the water because I feel like shark bait on the surface. And I really feel like shark bait today— because we're out in the deep water, miles offshore. The big bitey-guys live out here, though that thought quickly dissipates as I get closer to the whales.

I stop swimming and rest on top of the water in awe. Dolphins swim all around me, and whales spin under me. What a once-in-a-lifetime sight! I'm resting on the surface before getting the courage to swim underwater. It's such a weird feeling. I love to snorkel. What's my problem? I'm so excited. Why am I so scared at the same time? I know the whales will not hurt me; they are just so big that it is overwhelming. Snorkeling next to the coral reef, where I can see the bottom and even touch it, feels safer. But here, there's no bottom. The water is just never-ending blue. The way the bright sunlight hits the water creates light beams, which widen and then narrow into an inviting apex.

I'm alone, yet not. I'm afraid of swimming down while taking pictures—and not knowing how far I've gone. Normally, I gauge my depth relevant to the ocean floor. There's no way to measure my depth because there's no ocean floor here, or so it seems. My fear derives from swimming down without fins—and then not having enough air in my lungs to surface. My imagination conjures up a shallow-water blackout on the way up. I'd pass out swimming back up. Then I'd drop the camera and drown. Not a pretty thought.

While I'm having these defeatist thoughts on the surface, my legs are relaxed into a V-shape. Grant is back on the boat watching me and the dolphins all around me. He sees the most extraordinary thing happen; one curious dolphin swims very slowly toward me from behind, unbeknownst to me, and gently swims between my legs. Later, Grant says if he'd had a video camera, he could have filmed National Geographic footage, for sure. He thinks about calling out my name, but he knows if I turn around and see the fin, I might think it's a shark's fin and flip out. He can't believe the dolphin hasn't touched me and that I haven't moved my legs and accidentally kicked its snout.

I get my courage up, lift my head and take a deep breath. I swim down into the blue depths, shooting pictures of the whales. After resting on top of the water and not passing out, I notice the two whales are also resting for a moment deep down. As I watch, dolphins swim down and touch the nose of each whale. I blink inside my mask. If I could rub my eyes, I would. It's not a mistake, because the dolphins continue their little game. It looks as though they are almost bouncing off of each whale's nose. Hmmmm . . . a whale doesn't really have a nose. Okay, the dolphins were touching the top part of each whale's head, the part in front of the blowhole.

The whales tire of the game. They swim together and around each other upright, like ballroom dancers, creating the most synchronized beautiful waltz. I wish I had the video camera. I forget to take any pictures as I etch the experience into my mind and every sense of my body. It's a sensual ballet, the essence of love.

After watching the two whales repeatedly perform the submersed dance, I emerge for air, and the whales follow suit. The three of us rest, floating. Two dolphins pose near a whale's pectoral fin, stopping as if to say, "Here is your perfect picture, Patty. Take it." So, I do.

It's the last shot on the camera. I see a fast movement in the distance. Turning into my periphery, two dolphins quickly approach from my left. I'm so happy! I have been chasing these guys around the world, jumping in the water with them to convince them to play. Now, they are coming to me, without the chase, adding another Wow! moment to an already incredible day. I lift my head and start talking to them. I honestly believe they will understand my words. Why is it that when I see dolphins, I lose all sense of logic?

"Hey guys, the camera quit. I gotta swim back to the boat. Wanna' come with me?"

I can touch them; they are so close. I don't want to try, though, for fear it will scare them, spurring them to swim away. I quickly look away from the dolphins to briefly orient my eyes toward the boat, keeping my head turned to the side, so I can see the dolphins swimming directly beside me. I feel like we're in the same family. We don't need to talk to communicate. It's an understanding I can't explain—beautiful and bizarre.

They are so close. I can't contain my giddiness at having them near me. I finally tear myself away and turn my head forward to see how close I'm getting to the boat. As soon as I turn my head, I see it.

It is huge, a thick bronze leviathan swimming side to side, emerging from the depths. My life is over. My next thought is . . . the camera. I want Grant to have my photos if I'm going to be eaten by a shark. I'm still too far away from the boat. I quickly calculate the speed of the shark and the distance back to the boat. I'm not gonna' make it. I don't want to go this way!

"Grant!" I scream, desperate with panic, camera held high in the air. "Get the camera! Get the camera! Get the camera!"

My dolphin friends are no longer beside me. Vanished. The shark comes in for the kill. I feel like a skydiver whose chute has failed to open, velocity and inevitability hurtling me toward my death. I only have a few seconds of life left. *Dolphin Diver* is beside me. Grant races to the side of the boat, and I stretch my arm even higher, while firmly gripping the camera. I don't want the camera to fall into the sea on the shark's first bite.

Grant grabs my wrist, instead of the camera, bending his body over the side of *Dolphin Diver* so far that he could easily meet my same fate. It's not physically possible to do what he does. He pulls me out of the water with such force that I fly into the boat, doing a somersault twice over. Of course, I protect the camera in the process. I'm hyperventilating.

"It was a HUGE shark!" I say, between sucks of breath. "The dolphins . . . left me . . . " Now, I'm crying. Grant holds me there in a heap on the deck of the boat. I'm talking gibberish. He calms me, his eyes filling with tears. It takes a long time for me to calm down and realize I'm still here. I survived a shark attack.

After the fear subsides and I start breathing normally, I chatter like a child.

"Did you see the whales? Oh God, it was beautiful. Like a humpback ballet. And then those dolphins came along. It was like they were my friends. We talked about those big ole whales. And they posed for me! Did you see? Then they were swimming so close. Did you see?" Grant steers the boat back toward the harbor now and nods at all the right points in my story. There will be no fishing today.

I get sad. "Then they swam away. Can't say as I blame them . . . In fact, it was a pretty smart thing to do."

Grant, finally frustrated with my naiveté, stops the boat to put his hands on my shoulders, squaring my body with his. He looks deeply into my eyes with his piercing blue eyes and asks me: "You really don't know what happened back there, do you?"

In my defensive style, I say, "Of course I do . . . I was the one who almost got eaten by a SHARK! And you saved my ass!"

He smiles at my feistiness, as he has done so many times before. Then he takes a step back.

"As a matter of fact, your dolphin friends never left you at all. As I was coming up in the boat, I saw them swim away from you at top speed, smacking into that shark with two hard blows. Those dolphins saved your life, Patty. You were too far from the boat. If they hadn't been protecting you, you wouldn't be here."

They weren't being my friends. They were my protectors. Now, I know why they swam over to me and stayed so close. They knew what was happening long before I did.

We sit in silence for a long time. Before we enter the channel of the harbor, Grant turns off the boat and lets it drift with the breeze. We take a moment to look out to sea. And up to the heavens. In thanks. ■

POSSIBILITY Coaching Session

Living your life with an attitude of gratitude is a choice. The choice is all yours, and you can make that choice today.

Let's start by taking a look at what you are grateful for—especially the things you take for granted. Start with the basics that most of us don't even think about. Did you walk into your office on two legs? Did you drive your car to work today? Did you think about the importance of the depth perception that your two good eyes allow? Or the two good arms that allow you to steer? Do you have a voice and the ability to communicate with others? Do you smell the first cup of coffee in the morning before you even taste it? Do you feel warmth and love from a simple hug? All of these are examples of reasons to be grateful for, if you choose to be. Alternatively, you can just take it all for granted until you are forced to look at life differently.

> ┌─ VOGANISM ─┐
>
> We only have this very moment. How do you choose to spend it?"

Have you ever reflected on the fact that we have two ears and one mouth? You have been given the gift to listen twice as much as you talk. How often do you exercise this gift?

When you feel stressed or overwhelmed, take a moment to stop and count your blessings. When you feel the warmth of the sun on your face or the coolness of a gentle breeze, you will remember to have an attitude of gratitude for the gifts God has already given us. It is impossible to have a bad attitude if you choose to have an attitude of gratitude.

Discover Your POSSIBILITY Moments

As well as having an attitude of gratitude, the previous story is about recognizing the Possibility Moments in your life. When I saw all those dolphins in the water, even though it wasn't on the agenda and I wasn't totally prepared, I felt as though the ocean had brought me a gift, and I needed to acknowledge that gift by jumping in the water and playing with my water-loving friends. And look what happened! There was even more possibility in the moment, when the whales showed up, too. If I had been too focused on my own agenda, I never would have recognized the opportunity the universe was presenting to me.

How many Possibility Moments do you miss in your fast-paced, over-scheduled, full-of-responsibilities life? You owe it to yourself and the universe to recognize that each moment is full of unscheduled potential. You can choose to live your life glued to your to-do list and your scheduled tasks, or you can be connected and present right now, right here, where you are, and discover the possibility of each moment. I realize that we can't all live in the moment every single day. The challenge is to have enough flexibility—in your schedule, in your thinking, in your attitude—to be able to stop every once in a while and say, "You know what? I'm going to just enjoy the gift of this moment."

One perfect example comes from how you deal with another person, whether that person is an employee, a spouse, or a child. When you schedule a meeting with employees, do you allow the employee to bring their own concerns, issues, and ideas to the table? Sometimes the off-topic conversations you have with co-workers—whether the conversations are about work or about personal life—can be some of the most valuable and productive features of the meeting. The parent of any teenager knows that the best talks come when the teenager wants to share. If the teen starts talking, toss your schedule, because if you postpone this one, well, that opportunity is not likely to come up again soon.

Is your life so busy? Are you so consumed by your goals and your to-do list that Possibility Moments are passing you by daily, and you are not even noticing them? My guess is that your answer to this question is yes. If you cannot describe a moment within the past week when you derailed your agenda and veered in another direction because of a possibility that arose, you are most likely too busy, missing out on many great gifts.

As I write this section of the book, I am sitting in a café overlooking a little harbor in sunny California. The setting could not be more perfect. The Possibility Moment for me is NOT the stunning view, the warmth of the sun caressing my back, the kiss of the soft ocean breeze on my face, nor the reggae band plucking at my heart strings. It's the love displayed among family members who surround me. It's Father's Day. I am alone, not with my dad today. However, instead of feeling saddened by those around me who are with their fathers, I am discovering the possibility of this moment by enjoying the joy my heart feels, as I've chosen to stop, watch, and experience the love being experienced by others.

So many times, I have watched divers fiddle-farting around with their gear as they are sinking underwater. They aren't paying attention to what is happening around them. Thus, they hit precious coral and break off 100 years of growth, destroying the coral in seconds.

We, as leaders, can be just like the diver at times. We're self-centered, so busy looking at how everything is affecting us, that we could be doing damage to others without even realizing it until something is completely broken, just like the coral. Where are you showing up in your life like a non-observant, sinking diver?

When we're non-observant and sinking without being aware, we could be doing a great deal of damage to our employees and our businesses, not to mention our families. The reason this is so similar to scuba diving is that a diver can be sinking and not "feel" a thing because of the weightlessness. As a leader, you could be the primary factor in the problems within your business or family—and not even be aware until the damage has been done. So, many leaders have said these words: "I just didn't see it coming."

Here is one quick and simple awareness question for you to ask yourself. You can ask your employees, co-workers, and family members, too. Are you encouraging your employees to be creative and productive, or are you ignoring them because they are doing a good job and you "think" they are happy and fulfilled? You could be sinking slowly and breaking people down just like the unobservant diver broke the coral. Status quo is a silent deadly killer. Lack of action can destroy just as quickly as a great deal of action. Total lack of self-awareness is the beginning of the end.

Well, that is a very grim thought, isn't it? The good news is that the choice is all yours. You get to choose the type of leader you are today and the type of leader you are striving to become. Great scuba divers are like great leaders, aware of themselves and their surroundings at all times—and very protective of their precious ocean.

I have many favorite sayings and inspirational thoughts. One of the most important for me is so critical in discovering my possibility that I hope you find it to be just as powerful. You'll find it in the Voganism below. ■

VOGANISM

The stories you believe about yourself can make or break you; create your own new story of possibility.

Additional Important Reflections

Keep your THOUGHTS full of possibility
Because your thoughts
Become your WORDS.

Keep your WORDS positive
Because your words
Become your ACTIONS.

Keep your ACTIONS open to possibility
Because your actions
Become your HABITS.

Keep your HABITS positive
Because your habits
Become your VALUES.

Keep your VALUES true to possibility
Because your values
Define your PURPOSE.

The END . . . Is Just the BEGINNING

I always felt as though I would just know when it was time. Although I knew that strategic planning was important in a business, and I recognized that creating an exit strategy was even more important, I jumped into my business with both feet and left out these important parts. My intuition and Possibility Thinking drove this Tongan adventure from the moment I decided to attempt it seven years earlier, and I knew it would end the same way. Something would just tell me it was time to go.

That doesn't mean I didn't set goals every step of the way. From the very beginning, when I was determined to get through to the Tongan government for my business and development license, to build the shop, even though the cement mixer didn't work, to get the boat I wanted, I was determined to achieve my goals. Even though I did not know how or when Dolphin Pacific Diving would end, when my gut finally told me it was time, the first thing I did was establish a series of steps I would need to take to make that happen, to set simple and specific, timed and trackable, achievable and accountable, realistic and rewarding goals for the next stage in my journey.

And that's what it was to me, not an ending, but the beginning of a new journey.

. . . .

The stench wafts up, grabs my nose, and twists it like my big brother used to do. Yuck! I can't get rid of the smell. In fact, it is so pervasive that I feel as though it is permanently tattooed on my body.

Where does it come from? There is only one place on this isolated tropical island to get fuel for the boats: Don Coleman's fuel dock. The Shell Oil fuel boat does not stop at our small group of islands very often, certainly not on any regular schedule. In fact, sometimes Don totally runs out of fuel. On one occasion, the drought lasted about three years! Not really, but it sure felt that long!

Luckily, Don always calls and gives me a heads-up when he is low on fuel. He even fills 20-liter cans and puts them off to the side, so I can pick them up after returning my diver guests to the resort.

When Don runs out, the only other place on the island to get fuel is the petrol station way out near the airport. When that happens, about every third day, I put twelve empty petrol cans in the back of my dirty brown, broken-down pickup truck and drive on the dusty road, so full of potholes that it feels like a really bad ride at the County Fair. I fill each 20-liter can, then mix in the outboard engine oil. The motor oil and petrol create the stench I can never get off of my hands.

I drive back into town, the cans clattering in the back of the truck; then I carry two cans at a time down two flights of stairs to the dock. I do a balancing act to get the heavy, smelly, slippery cans into my dinghy, then I row four cans and one smelly me out to the big boat. The trick is to transfer the cans from the dinghy onto the big boat without falling into the water. I lift a 20-liter can and pour the petrol into a funnel that leads into the gas tank of the boat. Invariably, I splash petrol everywhere, including all over myself. By the time I get all twelve cans transferred, I am frustrated and exhausted, and I reek!

After seven years and hundreds of excursions, tasks like this just aren't fun anymore, and I'm starting to recognize the signs that it is time for me to end this adventure. I used to set goals for this task—complete it in the shortest time ever, for instance—and I always rewarded myself once I got it all done. But that's not working the way it used to, and I just feel tired.

I try to figure out what is exhausting me. Dolphin Pacific Diving is at the top of its game—at least the game I'm in right now. I originally started a dive business, then expanded into whale watching and then sport fishing. Eventually, I opened a booking office for all water sports. Then we expanded the booking office into a communication and business center for tour operators, locals, and world cruisers. Even the government officials come in to use the copy or fax machines. And most importantly, we went through the arduous process of acquiring a business license to operate each new section of the business. So yes, I would say, we are doing well.

But what's next? If I am going to grow this business even more, I need to buy a third boat to keep up with the sport fishing demand. And it would be smart to build a resort to house all my guests. But that's where I draw the line in the sand. I really don't want to get into building and running a resort. I just don't have enough energy left for that.

So instead, I figure it will take a minimum of two years to sell Dolphin Pacific Diving, Whale Watching, and Sport Fishing. Throughout the last seven years, I've been marketing in Australia, New Zealand, Canada, and North America.

Sometimes I got help from the Tongan Tourism board, sometimes Grant helped out, and in North America, my biggest fan, my dad, was always by my side. Before my last marketing trip to the US, I hired a general manager, a beautiful, highly organized British woman named Karen. (I just love the way the British sound when they talk even when they are telling you off, it still sounds so genteel! Perfect for customer service.)

One of the reasons I needed a general manager was that I had to fire myself. I was so burned out that I was overreacting to everything. I was letting F.E.A.R. (False Evidence Appearing Real; see Lesson 4) run my life, but the F.E.A.R. was totally irrational. I was suddenly terrified that someone would die on one of my boats. I'd been in business for six-and-a-half years without a single diving accident, much less a fatality. Instead of celebrating that, I was convinced that our luck was running out and something horrible was going to happen any day. I was freaking out so badly that I was no longer making rational decisions. If a slightly stronger current or the wind came up at all, I would end a dive early or cancel it altogether. It was clear that I needed to get some perspective and deal with my F.E.A.R.

POSSIBILITY COACHING TIP:

Today, I would not be so harsh; I would partner with the employee and coach them to figure out what is going on and the best action steps to take to have mutual benefit for the employee and the company. We would partner together in coming up with Possibility Solutions.

If I'd had an employee who acted as I was acting, I would have fired them in a New York minute. So, I took myself off of the scuba diving boats and confined myself to the office. I did go out on the whale watching trips, but it was the end of the season, so the trips were few and far between.

I extended a trip to the U.S., so I could figure out what was going on in my head. With a little distance from the business, I realized that my gut was telling me it was time to sell. I started this business because my gut told me to do it, and now my gut was telling me to get out. I couldn't do anything but listen.

One of the many challenges was finding a value for my company and pricing it to sell. The lessons I learned from the beautiful Tongan people and the stunning islands that were my home for many years, I would not trade for any amount of money. Being the first scuba diver to discover some of the underwater caves, swimming with a newborn baby humpback whale, having fish become my friends and allowing me to pet them underwater, being saved from a fatal shark attack by two dolphins—these were only a few of the adventures that no amount of money could buy. The life lessons of perseverance, friendship, determination, and love were also priceless. And most importantly, the Tongan people taught me to live my life through Possibility Thinking. They used creativity to overcome obstacles, stayed focused on the amazing blessings they had, rather than the things they lacked, and they always emphasized the importance of family, love, and relaxation. My time in Tonga had truly changed my view of what was really important in life.

As when I started the business, I set goals that moved me to the result that I desired. So I laid out a plan, with steps along the way, to seek a buyer and finalize a deal. Although I expected it to take a minimum of two years to sell the business, I was out and on my way back to my life in the States in only three months. That's because I took the time to set goals, and then I stuck to them. ∎

POSSIBILITY Coaching Session

It may seem strange that I cover goal setting in the last coaching session of my book; however, I'm hoping that for you, my reader, this is not the end, but the beginning. I hope you've learned about the power of Possibility Thinking and are ready to set goals to achieve your dreams. The end of anything is truly also the beginning of something else, and I hope this is true for you at the end of this book.

Now that I have been a business coach and Vistage Chair for years, I have walked a large variety of chief executives and business owners through the process of goal setting, strategic planning, and exit strategies. Flying by the seat of your pants and gut level intuition have their place, but if you want to live your life and run your business by design, instead of default, choosing to set goals will make the difference.

Like most people connected to the sea, the Tongans use celestial navigation to make their way from one island to another. In other words, they steer by the stars. For instance, the North Star shining in the sky is a guiding light for the North Pole, just as the Southern Cross points to the South Pole. In fact, as I gazed at the stars in Tonga, the Southern Cross became a friend to me while I looked up into the heavens and contemplated my goals for my business and my life.

This led me to create my own acronym for the qualities of effective goals: STAR goals.

STAR Goals are:

- S Simple and Specific
- T Timed and Trackable
- A Achievable and Accountable
- R Realistic and Rewarding

S: WRITE GOALS THAT ARE SIMPLE AND SPECIFIC

This creates goals that are easy to comprehend and easy to state aloud. When we speak our goals aloud, they become very powerful. The things we want to happen in our lives become real. If we use Possibility Thinking and speak as if our goals have already been achieved, then we may reach our goals even faster. (I know this sounds really weird, but it works.)

Examples:

- Business—Non-specific: *Everybody needs to step it up and get more sales and do better by the end of the second quarter.*

- Business—Simple and Specific: *We will increase sales by 15 percent by the end of the second quarter on X product.*

- Personal—Non-Specific: *I will lose weight and get healthy.*

- Personal—Specific and Simple: *I will be 20 pounds lighter by the end of the year. I will say these words aloud three times a day until the end of the year: I am a vision of health.*

T: CREATE A TIME FRAME AND MAKE YOUR GOAL TRACKABLE

Set a start date and an end date. Create milestones to keep yourself on track and to maintain the goal as your navigational tool, so you know you are going in the right direction each day. If you are not going in the right direction, adjust the goal as you would adjust your course.

Example:

- Create a Progress Sheet with monthly, weekly, and/or daily targets:

  Time Frame: 3 months

  Begin: April 1st

  End: June 30th or sooner

A: MAKE SURE YOUR GOALS ARE ACHIEVABLE AND THAT YOU AND/OR OTHERS ARE ACCOUNTABLE FOR ACHIEVING THEM

Having an accountability partner or team for business and personal goals is essential. We sometimes call that person a champion; it's like having a coach in your corner. With your accountability partner, answer these questions about your goal:the right direction, adjust the goal as you would adjust your course.

Who are you accountable to?
What are you trying to achieve?
When will you meet to talk about your progress?
Where will you meet?

Have a DOA (Direct, Open, and Authentic) Conversation about the goal. Remember, when you do NOT use DOA Communication, your intentions will be DOA (Dead On Arrival). That is the place where misunderstanding lives and grows like a disease.

Examples:

- Who: *I am responsible for meeting my goal, and I will report to the president on a weekly basis.*

- What: *The vice president of sales and I will work together to create benchmarks to meet this goal.*

- When: *The vice president of marketing and I will meet on the 15th of every month to review the milestones and make adjustments.*

- Where: *We will meet in my office.*

R: YOUR GOALS NEED TO BE REALISTIC

You need to really think about what you can achieve in the time frame you've set up. It is also helpful if your goals are measurable, as this provides another way to gauge whether they are realistic. Ask important questions.

Examples:

- *Have we given ourselves enough time to make this goal really happen? How do we know?*

- *What can get in our way of success?*

- *What will we do when we get off track?*

> ### VOGANISM
>
> Set your
>
> goals;
>
> step out
>
> and be
>
> bold.
>
> Begin
>
> now.
>
> Don't wait!
>
> The end …
>
> is just the
>
> beginning.

- *Have we done enough research—or too much? (Is it time to get on with it?)*
- *Do we have the tools we need?*
- *Are our benchmarks clearly defined so they will be helpful to evaluate our progress?*
- *Is the goal too big or too small?*
- *Is it challenging enough?*
- *Have we applied Possibility Thinking to the goals?*

Goals also need to be Rewarding. Ahhhh … the prize! Make it worthwhile. Take inventory of yourself or your team, and find out what team members think would be a motivating reward. Believe it or not, rewards do not always need to revolve around money, and your ideas are not always the best.

EPILOGUE

My Wish for You…

My wish for you is that when you put down this book, you will have the tools you need to experience the joy of discovering and exploring your own Possibility Driven Life.

Believe in yourself and open your mind, your heart, and your soul. Believe in *Possibility*, and discover a new chapter of adventure in life. You do not need to run away to a tropical island to do it. The answers are in your own backyard.

I am constantly discovering new possibilities in my life, and I find the answers closer to my heart each time. They are waiting for you, too; go get them!

The End …

is

just

the

Beginning.

Index

"Innovation is the key to staying ahead of the game in business. Patty has an uncanny ability to use common sense methods and make them feel like brand new ideas."

—*Bob McKnight, CEO of Quiksilver*

"In life there are influential people who come to you when you're standing at a crossroads. Patty Vogan is one of those influential people that you hope you get a return visit from. She will challenge you and make you think perhaps deeper than you are comfortable going, and that's exactly why she is such a precious gift."

—*Ryan Heuser the founder of Paul Frank Industries*

"They say don't judge a book by its cover, but in this case I recommend you do. This book's design is the perfect complement to Patty's captivating storytelling. She shares a fresh approach to understanding leadership, based on her own creative and courageous experiences. As Patty forcefully reminds us in her book (and as she has consistently shown her Vistage members): It's not about what we do, it's about who we are. Patty's learnings are worth absorbing for anyone who recognizes that leadership is not only about competence; it's about character."

—*Rafael Pastor, Chairman of the Board and CEO, Vistage International, Inc.*

"Patty's adventures are a metaphor for how we live, love, and lead. Her journey is our journey, and through her lens we see our greatest opportunities to embrace life and live it to our fullest. She has the talent and chutzpah to venture into experiences that we can all learn and benefit from. You go, girl!!"

—*Mikki Williams, CSP, professional speaker, coach, author, radio and TV personality*

"As Patty Vogan makes her own dreams come true in Tonga, she opens our eyes to the possibilities of the realization of our own dreams as well. Read Patty's magical book and you'll find your Tonga. I found mine!"

—*Michael Allosso, Executive Coach/Keynote Speaker*

About the author

Patty Vogan is the founder of Victory Coaching International, a leadership and communications training company based in San Clemente, CA who serve clients all over the globe. A Southern California native, Patty fulfilled a childhood dream when she moved to the South Pacific and the Kingdom of Tonga to open a scuba diving shop and sport fishing/whale watching tour business. She successfully operated the business for seven years before selling.

After returning to CA, she served as vice president of business development for the Ocean Institute, where she helped to raise more than $16 million in capital to build an educational facility for children to learn about science and become stewards of the ocean. Today she helps CEOs, Executives, and Teams by empowering leaders and individuals to achieve their full potential in business and life.

A celebrated speaker and author, Patty Vogan inspires audiences worldwide with her fun loving style and candid sharing of life experiences. Her natural ability to relate to people from all walks of life ensures her message and lessons have a lasting impact. Patty's first motivational book, "Surf-VIVAL Handbook for Land & Sea," was released in 2006 and used surfing as a metaphor for life.

Patty earned a Master's Degree in Psychological Sciences, remains very active as the Past President of the Monarch Beach Sunrise Rotary and has been involved in numerous philanthropic organizations that are dedicated to partnering with leaders for the betterment of our world. She balances her time to enjoy her favorite outdoor activities which include flying, sailing, surfing, golfing, cycling, scuba diving, photography, and her latest adventures are competitive ballroom dancing and outrigger canoeing.

1) QUICK TO LISTEN
2) SLOW TO SPEAK
3) SLOW TO ANGER